REFLECTIONS

A COMPILATION OF REFLECTIONS OF SELECTED ĀYĀT FROM JUZ 1-30 OF THE NOBLE QUR'ĀN

AISHA ALTAF

Published by:

Unit No. E-10, 5, Jln SS 15/4G, Subang Square,
47500 Subang Jaya, Selangor, Malaysia
+603-7772-3156 (office) / +6017-399-7411 (mobile)
info@tertib.press
www.tertib.press
@tertibpress (Facebook & Instagram)

Author	:	Aisha Altaf
Editor	:	Norashikin Azizan
Cover designer	:	Fathima Huzaifa Hussain
Typesetter	:	Fathima Huzaifa Hussain

REFLECTIONS: A COMPILATION OF REFLECTIONS OF SELECTED AYAT FROM JUZ 1-30 OF THE NOBLE QURAN

First Edition: February 2023

Perpustakaan Negara Malaysia   Cataloguing-in-Publication Data

Aisha Altaf, 1988-
REFLECTIONS : A Compilation of Reflections of Selected Ayat
from Juz 1-30 of the Noble Quran /
ISBN 978-967-2844-04-4
1. Qur'an--Criticism, interpretation, etc.
2. Qur'an--Translating.
3. Qur'an--Appreciation.
4. Muslims--Conduct of life.
5. Religious life--Islam.
I. Norashikin Azizan, 1997-. II. Title.
297.12242

CONTENTS

PREFACE

All Praise is due to Allāh and blessings and salutations upon His Messenger and chosen servant, Muhammad ﷺ. It is from Allāh's immense favour and unlimited mercy that He has revealed the greatest Book, the Glorious Qur'ān, which is a healing for the hearts, nourishment for the souls, and enlightenment for the minds. It guides out of darkness into the light, provides answers to questions that humanity has always wondered about and gives solutions to everyday problems. It is indeed the ultimate source of guidance!

The Prophet ﷺ said, "The Book of Allāh, the Exalted and Glorious, is the rope of Allāh. He who follows it will be upon right guidance and he who abandons it will be upon error."[1]

In light of the above, we decided to compile this short book with brief points of reflection from each *Juz'* (part) of the Qur'ān. The reflection points are theme-based and pertinent to everyday matters covering a range of topics from worship, supplications, morals and ethics, sustenance, divine decree; to dealings with people.

This book is designed to enable the busy reader to easily find and benefit from some of the many lessons learned from the Qur'ān, in hopes, that it will be a source of spiritual, emotional and religious guidance.

A special note of gratitude to Ustazah Dr. Farhat Hashmi for being a constant source of inspiration and encouragement, and to all those who have contributed towards this book in any capacity. We ask Allāh to accept this work from us and make it a source of much benefit and goodness.

Aisha Altaf

---

[1]   Saḥīḥ Muslim

بِسْمِ ٱللَّهِ ٱلرَّحْمَٰنِ ٱلرَّحِيمِ

GRATITUDE
JUZ' 1 | AL-FĀTIHAH

بِسْمِ اللَّهِ الرَّحْمَنِ الرَّحِيمِ ۝ اَلْحَمْدُ لِلَّهِ رَبِّ الْعَالَمِينَ ۝ الرَّحْمَنِ الرَّحِيمِ ۝ مَالِكِ يَوْمِ الدِّينِ ۝ إِيَّاكَ نَعْبُدُ وَإِيَّاكَ نَسْتَعِينُ ۝ اهْدِنَا الصِّرَاطَ الْمُسْتَقِيمَ ۝ صِرَاطَ الَّذِينَ أَنْعَمْتَ عَلَيْهِمْ غَيْرِ الْمَغْضُوبِ عَلَيْهِمْ وَلَا الضَّالِّينَ ۝

(1) In the name of Allāh, the Entirely Merciful, the Especially Merciful. (2) [All] praise is [due] to Allāh, Lord of the worlds- (3) The Entirely Merciful, the Especially Merciful, (4) Sovereign of the Day of Recompense. (5) It is You we worship and You we ask for help. (6) Guide us to the straight path - (7) The path of those upon whom You have bestowed favor, not of those who have evoked [Your] anger or of those who are astray.

A beautiful lesson

Sūrah al-Fātiḥah teaches us the beautiful lesson of gratitude, the lesson of praising and glorifying our Lord:

ٱلْحَمْدُ لِلَّهِ رَبِّ ٱلْعَٰلَمِينَ ۝

[All] praise is [due] to Allāh, Lord of the worlds.
[al-Fātiḥah:2]

All praises, and every kind and type of praise belongs to Him, because whatever blessing we have is from Allāh!

وَمَا بِكُم مِّن نِّعْمَةٍ فَمِنَ ٱللَّهِ

And whatever you have of favor - it is from Allāh.
[an-Naḥl:53]

Everything is praising him

The entire creation is doing His *Ḥamd* (praise):

وَإِن مِّن شَىْءٍ إِلَّا يُسَبِّحُ بِحَمْدِهِۦ

And there is not a thing except that it exalts [Allāh] by His praise [al-Isrā':44]

The skies are praising Allāh, the earth is glorifying Him, every single thing: every tree, every rock is praising Him, it is just that we do not understand their way of exalting Him. So how excellent would it be that we wholeheartedly say: *Alḥamdulillāh*!

The Messenger of Allāh ﷺ said,

أَفْضَلُ عِبَادِ اللَّهِ يَوْمَ الْقِيَامَةِ الْحَمَّادُونَ

"The most superior servants on the Day of Judgment will be '*Ḥammādūn*' (i.e., those who praise and glorify Allāh abundantly)."[1]

1 as-Silsilah as-Saḥīḥah

Sūrah al-Fātiḥah is also a *du'ā* (supplication); it is a *du'ā* for seeking guidance:

ٱهْدِنَا ٱلصِّرَاطَ ٱلْمُسْتَقِيمَ ۝

Guide us to the straight path.

[al-Fātiḥah:6]

The need for guidance is greater than the need for anything else, because the one who attains guidance attains *taqwa* (piety), and the one who attains *taqwa*, then Allāh makes a way out for him and provides provision for him from where he does not even imagine:

وَمَن يَتَّقِ اللَّهَ يَجْعَل لَّهُ مَخْرَجًا ۝ وَيَرْزُقْهُ مِنْ حَيْثُ لَا يَحْتَسِبُ

And whoever fears Allāh - He will make for him a way out. And will provide for him from where he does not expect.

[at-Talāq:2-3]

Another supplication for guidance is:

اللَّهُمَّ اهْدِنِي وَسَدِّدْنِي

O Allāh guide me and keep me straight[1]

---

1 Saḥīḥ Muslim, Book 8 Hadith 104

SAKĪNAH

وَقَالَ لَهُمْ نَبِيُّهُمْ إِنَّ ءَايَةَ مُلْكِهِۦ أَن يَأْتِيَكُمُ ٱلتَّابُوتُ فِيهِ سَكِينَةٌ مِّن رَّبِّكُمْ وَبَقِيَّةٌ مِّمَّا تَرَكَ ءَالُ مُوسَىٰ وَءَالُ هَٰرُونَ تَحْمِلُهُ ٱلْمَلَٰئِكَةُ إِنَّ فِى ذَٰلِكَ لَأَيَةً لَّكُمْ إِن كُنتُم مُّؤْمِنِينَ ۝

(248) And their Prophet said to them, "Indeed, a sign of his kingship is that the chest will come to you in which is assurance from your Lord and a remnant of what the family of Mūsa and the family of Hārūn had left, carried by the angels. Indeed in that is a sign for you, if you are believers."

This *āyah* (verse) is described as the '*Āyah* of *Sakīnah*' (verse of tranquility).

Sakīnah is the contentment and peace that Allāh places in the hearts of His servants; it brings peace and tranquility to a person, it makes him calm, it gives him strength and courage at the time of fear, so *fitnah* (slander) does not shake him, tests do not distract him, grief does not consume him, and his *imān* (faith) and *yaqīn* (confidence) increases.

Ibn al-Qayyim ﷽ said about *sakīnah*: "This is a rank among the ranks that Allāh grants; this rank is not due to man's own effort and earnings."

Ibn al-Qayyim ﷽ also said: "Indeed Allāh mentioned '*as-Sakīnah*' (Tranquility) in His Book in six places: al-Baqarah: 248, al-Tawbah: 26, 40, al-Fatḥ: 4, 18, 26."

Ibn al-Qayyim ﷽ further says: "Shaykh Ibn Taimiyyah ﷽ used to read the *Āyāh* of *Sakīnah* if matters became intense for him. And I heard him talk about a great incident which occurred when he was sick, the general intellect is too deficient to comprehend how evil souls emerged and fought against him in his state of weakness.

Ibn Taimiyyah ﷺ said, 'When this matter became intense, I said to my relatives and those around me: 'Read the *Āyāt* of *Sakīnah*'. Then I became free from this condition, and I sat up as if a transformation had taken place and there was nothing wrong with me (i.e., the sickness was gone).'

Ibn al-Qayyim ﷺ said, 'I also tried this, and I read these *Āyāt* of *Sakīnah* when the heart becomes agitated due to what affects it and I witnessed the amazing effects of these *Āyāt* on the tranquility of the heart and its peacefulness.'"[1]

So any time you feel worried or restless, then start reciting these *āyāt*, *inshāAllāh* it will bring peace and calmness to the heart.

---

[1] Madarij as-Salikin

HEART MATTERS
JUZ' 3 | ĀLI-'IMRĀN

رَبَّنَا لَا تُزِغْ قُلُوبَنَا بَعْدَ إِذْ هَدَيْتَنَا وَهَبْ لَنَا
مِن لَّدُنكَ رَحْمَةً إِنَّكَ أَنتَ ٱلْوَهَّابُ ۝

(8) [Who say], "Our Lord, let not our hearts deviate after You have guided us and grant us from Yourself mercy. Indeed, You are the Bestower."

This *āyah* is a *du'ā* for the safeguarding and protection of the heart because the heart is one of the most important parts of the body.

The soundness of *imān* is based on the soundness of the heart. The place of *taqwa* (piety) is also the heart, and it is also the seed of perception and understanding.

And it is for this reason, we have been taught many supplications for the spiritual health of the heart, such as:

A Guided Heart

اللَّهُمَّ اهْدِ قَلْبِى وَسَدِّدْ لِسَانِى وَاسْلُلْ سَخِيمَةَ قَلْبِى

O Allāh! guide my heart, make true my tongue and draw out the malice of my chest.[1]

An Enlightened Heart

اللَّهُمَّ اجْعَلْ فِى قَلْبِى نُورًا

O Allāh, place light in my heart.[2]

A Firm Heart

يَا مُقَلِّبَ الْقُلُوبِ ثَبِّتْ قَلْبِى عَلَى دِينِكَ

O the One Who turns the hearts, make my heart firm on Your Religion.[3]

---

1   Sunan Abu Dawūd, Book 8 Hadith 95
2   Sunan Abu Dawūd, Book 5 Hadith 104
3   Jami' at-Tirmidhī, Book 48 Hadith 153

A Cleansed Heart

اللَّهُمَّ اغْسِلْ قَلْبِي بِمَاءِ الثَّلْجِ وَالْبَرَدِ وَنَقِّ قَلْبِي مِنَ الْخَطَايَا كَمَا نَقَّيْتَ الثَّوْبَ الْأَبْيَضَ مِنَ الدَّنَسِ

O Allāh, wash my heart with snow and hail water,
and cleanse my heart of sins as You cleanse a white garment of filth[4]

A Good Heart

اللَّهُمَّ إِنِّي أَعُوذُ بِكَ مِنْ شَرِّ سَمْعِي وَمِنْ شَرِّ بَصَرِي وَمِنْ شَرِّ لِسَانِي وَمِنْ شَرِّ قَلْبِي وَمِنْ شَرِّ مَنِيِّي

O Allāh, I seek refuge in You from the evil of my hearing, from the evil
of my seeing, from the evil of my tongue, from the evil of my heart, and
from the evil of my maniyy (i.e., sexual desires).[5]

An Adorned Heart

اللَّهُمَّ حَبِّبْ إِلَيْنَا الْإِيمَانَ وَزَيِّنْهُ فِي قُلُوبِنَا وَكَرِّهْ إِلَيْنَا الْكُفْرَ وَالْفُسُوقَ وَالْعِصْيَانَ وَاجْعَلْنَا مِنَ الرَّاشِدِينَ

O Allāh! Make faith dear to us and make it pleasing in our hearts and
make disbelief, defiance and disobedience hateful to us, and make us
among the rightly guided.[6]

These *du'ās* are essential and extremely beneficial, especially when one feels constriction of the heart!

---

4 Sunan an-Nasa'ī, Book 2 Hadith 9
5 Sunan Abu Dawūd, Book 8 Hadith 136
6 al-Adab al-Mufrad, Book 31 Hadith 96

THE HOUSE OF ALLĀH
JUZ' 4 | ĀLI-'IMRĀN

إِنَّ أَوَّلَ بَيْتٍ وُضِعَ لِلنَّاسِ لَلَّذِى بِبَكَّةَ مُبَارَكًا وَهُدًى لِّلْعَـٰلَمِينَ ۝

(96) Indeed, the first House [of worship] established for mankind was that at Bakkah (Makkah)-blessed and a guidance for the worlds.

Three points are mentioned about the House of Allāh at Makkah:

1) It was the first place of worship to be established on this earth.
2) It is blessed.
3) It is a means of guidance for the worlds.

The House of Allāh is blessed in a number of ways.

When you offer a *Salāh* (prayer) in your own home, the reward for that prayer equals ten rewards. But when you offer a prayer in Makkah, in *Baitullāh* (the House of Allah), the reward for that one prayer is 100,000 rewards!

The Prophet ﷺ said, "One prayer in my masjid is better than one thousand prayers elsewhere, except al-Masjid al-Ḥarām, and one prayer in al-Masjid al-Ḥarām is better than one hundred thousand prayers elsewhere."[1]

Similarly, the charity that you give, the Qur'ān that you recite, the *Tawāf* (circumambulation around Kaabah) that you do, the *Umrah* or *Ḥajj* (pilgrimage) that you perform, the reward for all these good deeds is multiplied manifold. This is *barakah* (blessing)!

The House of Allāh is also *Mubārak* (blessed) in the sense that making *Ḥajj* or *Umrah* to the House brings many benefits:

The Messenger of Allāh ﷺ said, "Make the *Ḥajj* and *Umrah* follow each other closely (i.e., keep on doing *Ḥajj* and *Umrah*), for they remove poverty

---

1   Sunan Ibn Majah, Book 5 Hadith 604

and sins as the bellows removes the impurities from iron, gold and silver, and an accepted *Ḥajj* brings no less a reward than Paradise."[2]

The journey to the House of Allāh might not be the easiest journey. One will spend his wealth on expenses and may also endure many types of hardships. In the olden days, the pilgrims travelled on camels and horses, enduring a different kind of hardship. Today's hardships are no less. Sometimes one has to wait for long hours in queues or experience the rush of people. But the sweetness of worship that you experience in the House of Allāh is totally worthwhile compared to all the hardships that you faced to get there.

This is why at least make the intention and resolve to visit the House of Allāh so that even if for some reason you are unable to, you will be rewarded for your intention!

May Allāh grant us the opportunity and ability to visit the House of Allāh.

THE GREETING OF PEACE

JUZ' 5 | AL-NISĀ

وَإِذَا حُيِّيتُم بِتَحِيَّةٍ فَحَيُّوا۟ بِأَحْسَنَ مِنْهَآ أَوْ رُدُّوهَآ إِنَّ اللَّهَ كَانَ عَلَىٰ كُلِّ شَىْءٍ حَسِيبًا ۝

(86) And when you are greeted with a greeting, greet [in return] with one better than it or [at least] return it [in a like manner]. Indeed, Allāh is ever, over all things, an Accountant.

The one who greets you, greet them in return; the one who does good to you, do good to them in return and here specifically the reference is towards the greeting of *salām* (greetings). When someone says the *salām* to you, respond to them with the *salām*.

The Prophet ﷺ said, "Verily, *As-Salām* is a Name among the Names of Allāh. He has ordained it on the earth, so spread the *salām* among yourselves."[1]

Spreading the greeting of *salām* brings peace

The Prophet ﷺ said, "Spread the greeting of peace and you will receive peace."[2]

It is a means of forgiveness

Hani' ibn Yazid ؓ reported, "I said, 'O Messenger of Allāh, show me a deed that will admit me into Paradise.' The Prophet ﷺ said, 'Verily, among the deeds that result in forgiveness is offering *salām* and good words.'"[3]

It is a means of increasing love

The Prophet ﷺ said, "By He in Whose Hand is my soul! You will not enter Paradise until you believe, and you will not believe until you love each other. Shall I direct you to something that, if you did, you would love each other? Spread the *salām* among yourselves."[4]

When you feel a lack of love in a relationship, then firmly hold on to this advice of the Prophet ﷺ. Spread the *salām* in abundance, as a result, love will increase and flourish, *InshaAllāh*. It will save you from great problems in family life as well.

When families spread the *salām* to each other, when the first thing the husband says to his wife when he wakes up and the wife to her husband when she wakes up is the *salām*, when parents give *salām* to their children and children to their parents, when they say *salām* when leaving the house and upon entering, then this will create a positive and pleasant environment, increases love, bringing peace into the family, *InshaAllāh*.

---

1   al-Adab al-Mufrad, Book 42 Hadith 25
2   al-Adab al-Mufrad
3   as-Silsilah as-Saḥīḥah
4   Saḥīh Muslim, Book Hadith 101

Initiating the greeting of salām

The Messenger of Allāh ﷺ said, "Verily, the best of people to Allāh are those who are first to greet with the salām."[1]

VIRTUES OF WUDŪ'
JUZ' 6 | AL-MĀ'IDAH

يَـٰٓأَيُّهَا ٱلَّذِينَ ءَامَنُوٓاْ إِذَا قُمْتُمْ إِلَى ٱلصَّلَوٰةِ فَٱغْسِلُواْ وُجُوهَكُمْ وَأَيْدِيَكُمْ إِلَى ٱلْمَرَافِقِ وَٱمْسَحُواْ بِرُءُوسِكُمْ وَأَرْجُلَكُمْ إِلَى ٱلْكَعْبَيْنِ وَإِن كُنتُمْ جُنُبًا فَٱطَّهَّرُواْ وَإِن كُنتُم مَّرْضَىٰٓ أَوْ عَلَىٰ سَفَرٍ أَوْ جَآءَ أَحَدٌ مِّنكُم مِّنَ ٱلْغَآئِطِ أَوْ لَـٰمَسْتُمُ ٱلنِّسَآءَ فَلَمْ تَجِدُواْ مَآءً فَتَيَمَّمُواْ صَعِيدًا طَيِّبًا فَٱمْسَحُواْ بِوُجُوهِكُمْ وَأَيْدِيكُم مِّنْهُ مَا يُرِيدُ ٱللَّهُ لِيَجْعَلَ عَلَيْكُم مِّنْ حَرَجٍ وَلَـٰكِن يُرِيدُ لِيُطَهِّرَكُمْ وَلِيُتِمَّ نِعْمَتَهُۥ عَلَيْكُمْ لَعَلَّكُمْ تَشْكُرُونَ ۝

(6) O you who have believed, when you rise to [perform] prayer, wash your faces and your forearms to the elbows and wipe over your heads and wash your feet to the ankles. And if you are in a state of *janabah* (impure), then purify yourselves. But if you are ill or on a journey or one of you comes from the place of relieving himself or you have contacted women and do not find water, then seek clean earth and wipe over your faces and hands with it. Allāh does not intend to make difficulty for you, but He intends to purify you and complete His favor upon you that you may be grateful.

By obligating *wudū'* (ablution) before *salāh*, Allāh intends to purify His servants, both physically and spiritually, and complete His favour upon them. A blessing for which we must be ever grateful!

Wudū' may seem like a simple act of washing specific limbs of the body, but it is actually an act of worship through which a person attains closeness to Allāh. It is half of *imān* (faith) and holds great virtues.

Adornment in Paradise

The Prophet ﷺ said, "The adornment of the believer (in Jannah) will reach the places where the water of *wudū'* reaches (his body)."[1]

A Means of Forgiveness

The Prophet ﷺ said, "None of you who uses water for ablution and rinses his mouth, sniffs up water and blows it, but the sins of his face, and his mouth and his nostrils fall out. When he washes his face, as Allāh has commanded him, the sins of his face fall out from the end of his beard with water. Then (when) he washes his forearms up to the elbows, the sins of his arms fall out along with water from his finger-tips. And when he wipes his head, the sins of his head fall out from the points of his hair along with water. And (when) he washes his feet up to the ankles, the sins of his feet fall out from his toes along with water. And if he stands to pray and praises Allāh, lauds Him and glorifies Him and shows wholehearted devotion to Allāh, his sins would depart leaving him (as innocent) as he was on the day his mother bore him."[2]

The Prophet ﷺ said, "He who performs *wudū'* perfectly (i.e., according to Sunnah), his sins will depart from his body, even from under his nails."[3]

Radiance on the Day of Judgment

The Companions said, "O Messenger of Allāh! How will you recognize those of your Ummah who are not born yet?" He ﷺ said, "Say, if a man has white-footed horses with white foreheads among horses which are pure black, will he not recognize his own horses?" They said, "Certainly, O Messenger of Allāh!" He ﷺ said, "They (my followers) will come with radiant faces and white limbs because of *wudū'*; and I will arrive at the *Ḥaud* (*Al-Kauthar*) ahead of them."[4]

---

1   Mishkat al-Masabih, Book 3 Hadith 10
2   Saḥīḥ Muslim
3   Saḥīḥ Muslim, Book 2 Hadith 45
4   Riyad as-Salihin, Book 8 Hadith 39

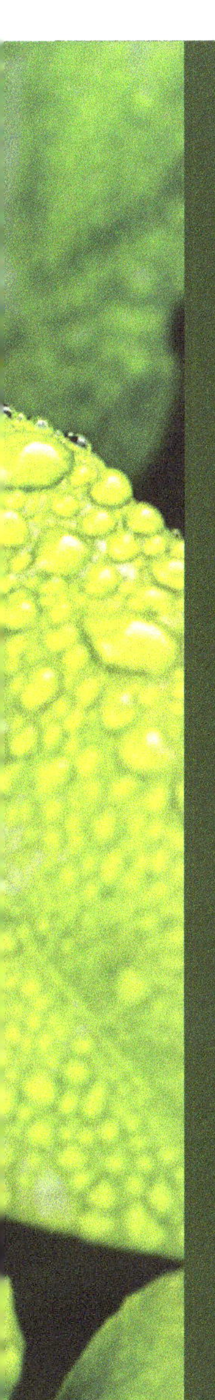

A WEEPING EYE

JUZ' 7 | AL-MĀ'IDAH

وَإِذَا سَمِعُواْ مَآ أُنزِلَ إِلَى ٱلرَّسُولِ تَرَىٰٓ أَعْيُنَهُمْ تَفِيضُ مِنَ ٱلدَّمْعِ مِمَّا عَرَفُواْ مِنَ ٱلْحَقِّ يَقُولُونَ رَبَّنَآ ءَامَنَّا فَٱكْتُبْنَا مَعَ ٱلشَّـٰهِدِينَ ۝ وَمَا لَنَا لَا نُؤْمِنُ بِٱللَّهِ وَمَا جَآءَنَا مِنَ ٱلْحَقِّ وَنَطْمَعُ أَن يُدْخِلَنَا رَبُّنَا مَعَ ٱلْقَوْمِ ٱلصَّـٰلِحِينَ ۝ فَأَثَـٰبَهُمُ ٱللَّهُ بِمَا قَالُواْ جَنَّـٰتٍ تَجْرِى مِن تَحْتِهَا ٱلْأَنْهَـٰرُ خَـٰلِدِينَ فِيهَا وَذَٰلِكَ جَزَآءُ ٱلْمُحْسِنِينَ ۝

(83) And when they hear what has been revealed to the Messenger, you see their eyes overflowing with tears because of what they have recognised of the truth. They say, "Our Lord, we have believed, so register us among the witnesses.   (84) And why should we not believe in Allāh and what has come to us of the truth? And we aspire that our Lord will admit us [to Paradise] with the righteous people."   (85) So Allāh rewarded them for what they said with gardens [in Paradise] beneath which rivers flow, wherein they abide eternally. And that is the reward of doers of good.

It is the way of the *Sāliḥīn* (righteous) to cry when they hear the *Kalām* (Speech) of Allāh. The Qur'ān has a direct effect on the hearts and the weeping eye is a sign of that. The tears that flow from the eye may seem to be something trivial, but every drop that is shed with sincerity out of Allah becomes a means of forgiveness!

The Prophet ﷺ said, "There are three types of people whose eyes will not see Hellfire: an eye which weeps out of fear of Allāh, the eye which is guarding in the cause of Allāh, and the eye which turns away from what Allāh has forbidden."[1]

The Prophet ﷺ said: "No man who weeps for fear of Allah will be touched by the Fire until the milk goes back into the udders. And the dust (of Jihad) in the cause of Allah and the smoke of Hell, will never be combined in the nostrils of a Muslim."[2]

This is to show impossibility. Just as it is not possible for milk to go back into the udder, it is impossible that such a person will enter the Fire, i.e., he will be saved from it.

May Allāh make us among the *Sāliḥīn* whose hearts are softened at the remembrance of Allāh.

---

1   as-Silsilah as-Saḥīḥah
2   Sunan an-Nasa'i, Book 25 Hadith 23

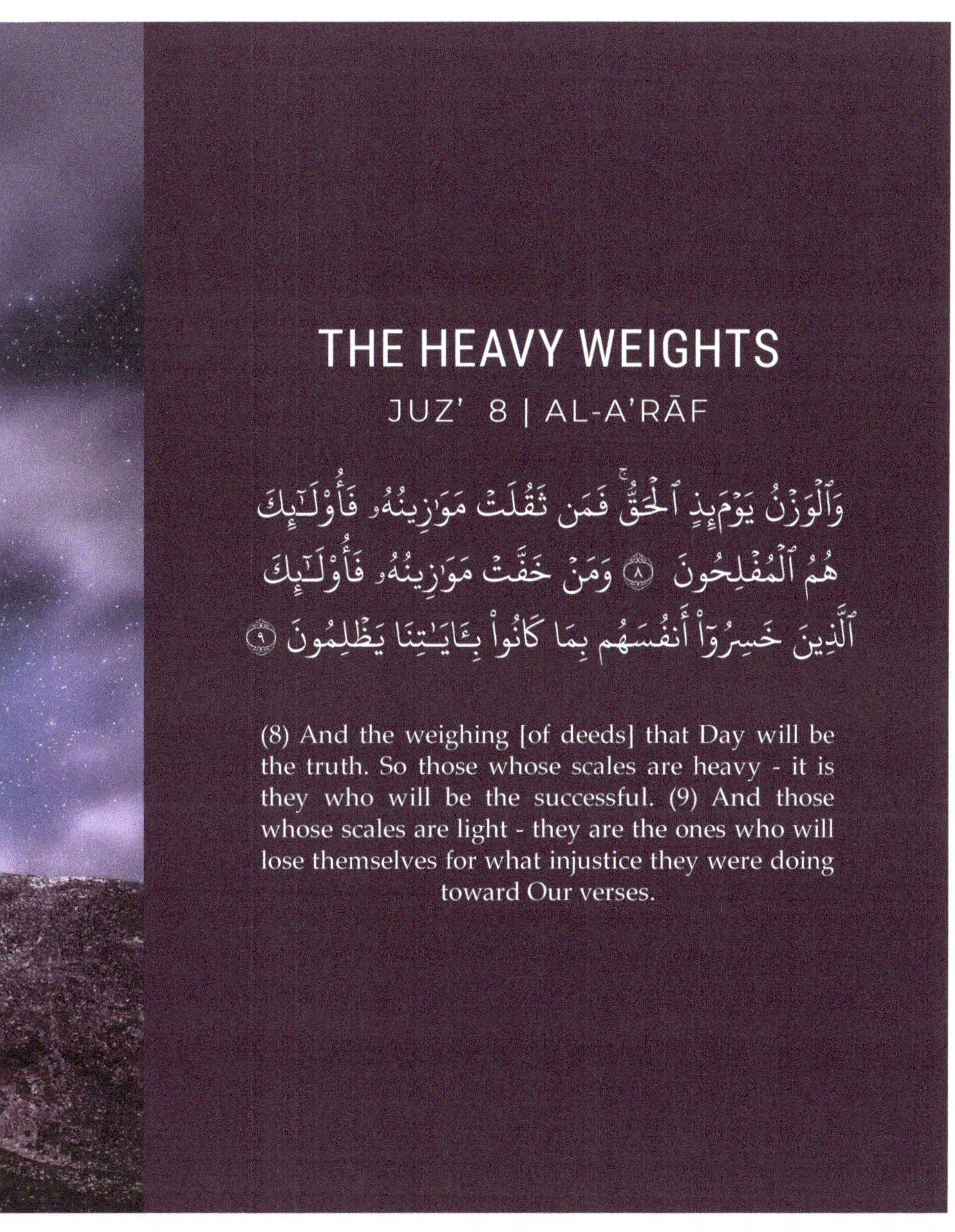

THE HEAVY WEIGHTS

JUZ' 8 | AL-A'RĀF

وَٱلْوَزْنُ يَوْمَئِذٍ ٱلْحَقُّ فَمَن ثَقُلَتْ مَوَٰزِينُهُۥ فَأُوْلَـٰٓئِكَ هُمُ ٱلْمُفْلِحُونَ ۝ وَمَنْ خَفَّتْ مَوَٰزِينُهُۥ فَأُوْلَـٰٓئِكَ ٱلَّذِينَ خَسِرُوٓاْ أَنفُسَهُم بِمَا كَانُواْ بِـَٔايَـٰتِنَا يَظْلِمُونَ ۝

(8) And the weighing [of deeds] that Day will be the truth. So those whose scales are heavy - it is they who will be the successful. (9) And those whose scales are light - they are the ones who will lose themselves for what injustice they were doing toward Our verses.

The weighing of deeds will definitely take place on the Day of Judgment. Actions will be weighed on the scales and so will the record of deeds.

The Scale is a real scale, whose vast size is known only to Allāh.

The Prophet ﷺ said, "During Resurrection Day, the Scales will be set up such that, even if the heavens and earth were to be weighed in them, they would accommodate them. The angels will say, 'Our Lord, whose deeds would be (so great as to be) weighed in these Scales?' Allāh will reply, 'Whoever's deeds I will from among my creation.' The angels will then say, 'Exalted are You! We surely have not worshiped you as much as You deserve.'"[1]

---

1   al-Ḥākim

The Heavy Weights

1. True and pure belief in Allāh

2. Good Manners

The Prophet ﷺ said, "Nothing is heavier upon the scale of the believer on the Day of Resurrection than his good character."[1]

3. Remembrance of Allāh

The Prophet ﷺ said, "There are two statements that are beloved to the Most Merciful, light on the tongue, and heavy on the Scales: *'SubḥānAllāhi wa-biḥamdihi, SubḥānAllāhil-'Adheem'* (Exalted is Allāh and praise be to Him, Exalted is Allāh, the Great)."[2]

The Prophet ﷺ said, "Purity is half of *Imān*, and *Alḥamdulillāh* fills the scale." [3]

The Prophet ﷺ said, "There are two deeds that a Muslim does not preserve except that he will enter Paradise. They are easy although those who practice them are few. It is to glorify Allāh (*SubḥānAllāh*) ten times and to praise Allāh (*Alḥamdulillāh*) ten times and to exalt Allāh (*Allāhu Akbar*) ten times at the end of every prayer, for it is one hundred and fifty upon the tongue but one thousand five hundred upon the scale. And it is to glorify Allāh (*SubḥānAllāh*) thirty three times and to praise Allāh (*Alḥamdulillāh*) thirty three times and to exalt Allāh (*Allāhu Akbar*) thirty four times when going to sleep, for it is one hundred upon the tongue and one thousand upon the scale."[4]

O Allāh make our Scales heavy on that Day!

---

1   Jami' at-Tirmidhī, Book 27 Hadith 109
2   Saḥīh Muslim, Book 48 Hadith 41
3   40 Hadith of Nawawi, Hadith 23
4   Sunan Ibn Majah, Book 5 Hadith 124

POWER OF ISTIGHFĀR

JUZ' 9 | AL-ANFĀL

وَمَا كَانَ ٱللَّهُ لِيُعَذِّبَهُمْ وَأَنتَ فِيكِمْ وَمَا كَانَ ٱللَّهُ مُعَذِّبَهُمْ وَهُمْ يَسْتَغْفِرُونَ ﴿٣٣﴾

(33) But Allāh would not punish them while you, [O Prophet], are among them, and Allāh would not punish them while they seek forgiveness.

One of the greatest blessings of our Lord is His Mercy and forgiveness. When a person sincerely turns back to His Lord seeking forgiveness, He will find His Lord Most Forgiving!

Istighfār (seeking forgiveness) is the solution to every problem, it is a means of removing obstacles, averting calamities, and earning the pleasure and love of Allāh and a means of increase in blessings and provision.

The Prophet ﷺ said, "Whoever gets up at night and says:

لاَ إِلَهَ إِلاَّ اللَّهُ وَحْدَهُ لاَ شَرِيكَ لَهُ

لَهُ الْمُلْكُ وَلَهُ الْحَمْدُ وَهُوَ عَلَى كُلِّ شَيْءٍ قَدِيرٌ

الْحَمْدُ لِلَّهِ وَسُبْحَانَ اللَّهِ وَلاَ إِلَهَ إِلاَّ اللَّهُ وَاللَّهُ أَكْبَرُ

وَلاَ حَوْلَ وَلاَ قُوَّةَ إِلاَّ بِاللَّهِ

'There is no deity worthy of worship except Allāh, alone is He, He has no partner. To Him belongs all sovereignty and praise and He is over all things competent. All praise is due to Allāh, exalted is Allāh and there is no deity worthy of worship except Allāh. Allāh is the Greatest, and there is no might nor power except with Allāh.'

And then says:

اللَّهُمَّ اغْفِرْ لِي

'O Allāh! Forgive me'

Or invokes (Allāh), he will be responded to and if he performs ablution (and prays), his prayer will be accepted." [1]

---

1   Ṣaḥīḥ al-Bukhārī, Book 19 Hadith 35

Ibn Umar ﷺ said, "In one sitting of the Messenger of Allāh ﷺ, one could count that he said a hundred times, before he would get up:"

رَبِّ اغْفِرْ لِي وَتُبْ عَلَيَّ إِنَّكَ أَنْتَ التَّوَّابُ الْغَفُورُ

"'O my Lord, forgive me and accept my repentance. Indeed, You are the Accepting of repentance, the Merciful."[1]

The Prophet ﷺ said, "There is no one who commits a sin then performs *wudū'* well and stands and prays two *rak'āt*, then asks Allāh for forgiveness, but Allāh will forgive him."[2]

`Abdullah bin Busr ﷺ narrated that a man said, "O Messenger of Allāh ﷺ there are many injunctions of Islam for me. So tell me something to which I may hold fast." He ﷺ said:

لاَ يَزَالُ لِسَانُكَ رَطْبًا مِنْ ذِكْرِ اللَّهِ

"Let not your tongue cease to be moist with the remembrance of Allāh."[3]

---

1   Jami' at-Tirmidhī, Book 48 Hadith 65
2   Sunan Ibn Majah, Book 5 Hadith 593
3   Jami' at-Tirmidhī, Book 48 Hadith 6

HEARTS UNITED

JUZ' 10 | AL-ANFĀL

وَأَطِيعُواْ ٱللَّهَ وَرَسُولَهُۥ وَلَا تَنَـٰزَعُواْ فَتَفْشَلُواْ وَتَذْهَبَ رِيحُكُمْ وَٱصْبِرُوٓاْ إِنَّ ٱللَّهَ مَعَ ٱلصَّـٰبِرِينَ ۝

(46) And obey Allāh and His Messenger, and do not dispute and [thus] lose courage and [then] your strength would depart; and be patient. Indeed, Allāh is with the patient.

This *āyah* (verse) tells us of the importance of not falling into disputes with one another. Disputes happen when people differ in their opinions and interests and become intolerant towards others.

There will be differences and different opinions, because differences are a part of life! Unity does not mean unification of opinions, it means that despite differences, people respect one another, tolerate each other, and refrain from disputes.

When we humble ourselves, put aside our differences, and come together in obedience to Allāh and His Messenger, while at the same time holding on to the Qur'ān and Sunnah, then this leads to harmony and unity. *United we stand, divided we fall.*

Repeatedly, we are told in the Qur'ān to be united as unity is the key to success, a means of strength, and a way to receive the mercy and help of Allāh. And it is the hearts especially that need to be united!

Abu Musa ﷺ narrated that the Prophet ﷺ said, "A believer to another believer is like the bricks of a wall, enforcing each other." The Prophet ﷺ then clasped his hands with the fingers interlaced (while saying that).[1]

---

1   Saḥīḥ al-Bukhārī, Book 8 Hadith 128

THE GREATEST BLESSING
JUZ' 11 | YŪNUS

يَٰٓأَيُّهَا ٱلنَّاسُ قَدْ جَآءَتْكُم مَّوْعِظَةٌ مِّن رَّبِّكُمْ وَشِفَآءٌ لِّمَا فِى ٱلصُّدُورِ وَهُدًى وَرَحْمَةٌ لِّلْمُؤْمِنِينَ ۝ قُلْ بِفَضْلِ ٱللَّهِ وَبِرَحْمَتِهِۦ فَبِذَٰلِكَ فَلْيَفْرَحُواْ هُوَ خَيْرٌ مِّمَّا يَجْمَعُونَ ۝

(57) O mankind, there has to come to you instruction from your Lord and healing for what is in the breasts and guidance and mercy for the believers. (58) Say, "In the bounty of Allāh and in His mercy - in that let them rejoice; it is better than what they accumulate."

Rejoice and be happy over the blessing of the Qur'ān for it is better than all that people accumulate of the things of this world.

If all the wealth and delights of this world were combined, they would be pale in comparison to the blessing of the Qur'ān, because the Qur'ān is the Word of Allāh. It is a healing and cure for the hearts, a source of guidance and mercy, and a means of goodness and prosperity. It prescribes abundant rewards in this world and the Hereafter.

For this reason, we should be ever grateful to Allāh for this blessing and maintain a strong connection with the Book, reading it, learning it and sharing it!

The Prophet ﷺ said, "There are people from the servants of Allāh who are neither Prophets nor martyrs; but the Prophets and martyrs will envy them on the Day of Resurrection for their rank with Allāh, the Most High." They (the people) asked, "O Messenger of Allāh ﷺ, who are they?" He ﷺ replied, "They are people who love one another for the Book of Allāh (i.e. the Qur'ān), without having any mutual kinship and transaction dealing. I swear by Allāh, their faces will glow and they will be (sitting) on (pulpits of) light. They will have no fear (on the Day) when the people will have fear, and they will not grieve when the people will grieve."

He ﷺ then recited the *āyah* where Allāh says:

$$\text{أَلَآ إِنَّ أَوْلِيَآءَ ٱللَّهِ لَا خَوْفٌ عَلَيْهِمْ وَلَا هُمْ يَحْزَنُونَ}$$

Unquestionably, [for] the allies of Allāh there will be no fear concerning them, nor will they grieve [Yūnus:62][1]

May Allāh make us of those who love each other for the Book of Allāh.

---

1 Sunan Abu Dawūd, Book 24 Hadith 112

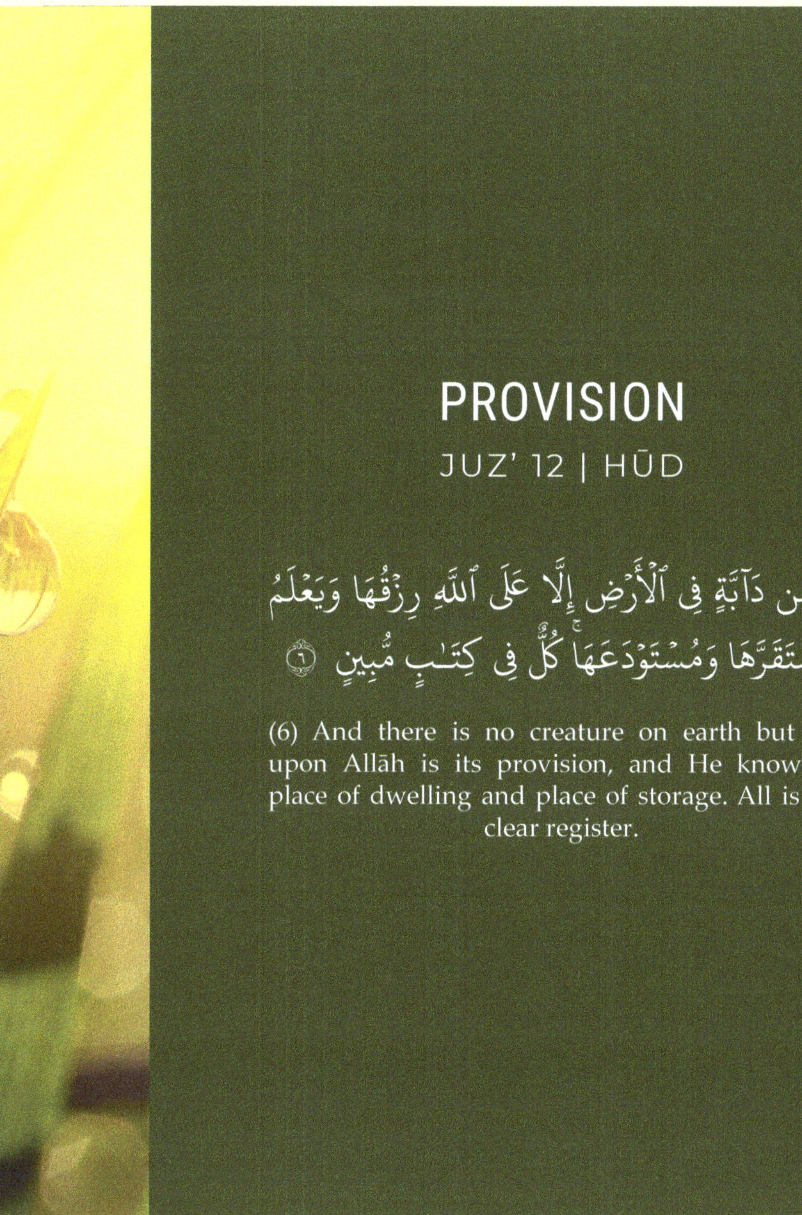

PROVISION
JUZ' 12 | HŪD

وَمَا مِن دَآبَّةٍ فِى ٱلْأَرْضِ إِلَّا عَلَى ٱللَّهِ رِزْقُهَا وَيَعْلَمُ مُسْتَقَرَّهَا وَمُسْتَوْدَعَهَا ۚ كُلٌّ فِى كِتَٰبٍ مُّبِينٍ ﴿٦﴾

(6) And there is no creature on earth but that upon Allāh is its provision, and He knows its place of dwelling and place of storage. All is in a clear register.

Allāh created the entire earth and also all that is on the earth of humans, *jinn* (spirit), animals, birds, fishes, and other creations. And Allāh did not just create them and leave them as they are, but also made arrangements for their provision: *"And there is no creature on earth but that upon Allāh is its provision."*

This is amazing! We have no knowledge about the different types of creatures that exist let alone their numbers, and the food that they consume, but Allāh provides for each one of them, He is the *Rāziq* (Provider).

The provision for each creature has already been decreed and it will definitely reach him: The Prophet ﷺ said, "If the son of Adam runs away from his provision just as he runs away from death, his provision will still come to him just as his death will come to him."[1]
It is from the immense bounty and favor of Allāh that He has arranged for the needs of the human being and it is for this reason, where on the one hand, we should work hard, but on the other, we should not worry too much about *rizq* (provision).

Instead, be more worried and concerned about deeds and preparing for the Hereafter, because the provision that is written for you here will definitely reach you.

---

1 as-Silsilah as-Saḥīḥah

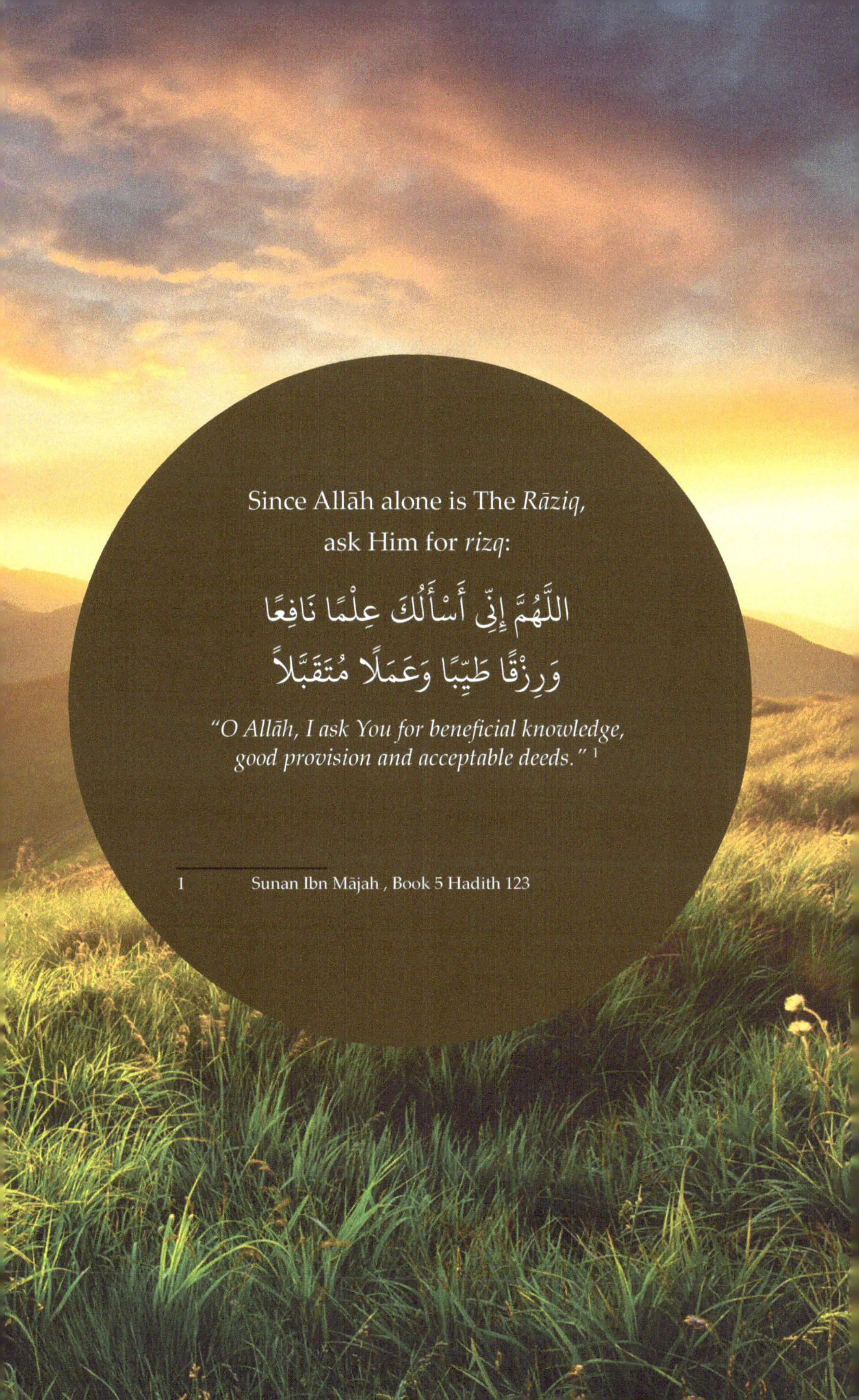

Since Allāh alone is The *Rāziq*,
ask Him for *rizq*:

اللَّهُمَّ إِنِّى أَسْأَلُكَ عِلْمًا نَافِعًا
وَرِزْقًا طَيِّبًا وَعَمَلًا مُتَقَبَّلاً

*"O Allāh, I ask You for beneficial knowledge,
good provision and acceptable deeds."* [1]

---

1   Sunan Ibn Mājah , Book 5 Hadith 123

FORGIVENESS

JUZ' 13 | YŪSUF

قَالَ لَا تَثْرِيبَ عَلَيْكُمُ ٱلْيَوْمَ يَغْفِرُ ٱللَّهُ لَكُمْ وَهُوَ أَرْحَمُ ٱلرَّاحِمِينَ ۝

(92) He said, "No blame will there be upon you today. Allāh will forgive you; and He is the most merciful of the merciful."

The story of Yūsuf is a story of many lessons. It is a beautiful story of a brother forgiving his brothers, brothers who had greatly wronged him, who took him away from his loving father and threw him into a well only to be picked up by a caravan and sold as a slave in Egypt, where he faced many hardships.

But Yūsuf did not dwell on the past. After all that his brothers had done to him, when he met them decades later as the minister of Egypt with the days of hardship long behind him, he did not even take a little bit of revenge!

The story of Yūsuf is a story of forgiveness! It is a story of patience and strength!

Benefits of forgiving others

1. Forgiveness of Sins

The Prophet ﷺ said, "He who does not show mercy to the people, Allāh does not show mercy to him, and he who does not forgive is not forgiven."[1]
If we are sincere in wanting Allāh to forgive us for our mistakes, we should be prepared to do that for others.

2. Increase in Honor

The Messenger of Allāh ﷺ said, "Charity does not decrease wealth, no one forgives another except that Allāh increases his honor, and no one humbles himself for the sake of Allāh except that Allāh raises his status."[2]

---

1   al-Adab al-Mufrad, Book 19 Hadith 10
2   Saḥīḥ Muslim, Book 45 Hadith 90

3. A Means of Emotional Strength and Happiness

The inability to forgive may cause a person to bring anger and resentment into relationships, harming himself and also others. But by pardoning, you are allowing yourself to let go of the past and move on, which paves the way for healing. You cannot change things that happen outside your control nor can you control people's behaviour. But you can control how you react and perceive it.

When you let go of resentment from clouding your judgment, you can then make peace with the past and move on. It is said: *Wisdom is born from a healed wound.*

You also feel more positive and relaxed when you forgive others as you have removed a burden from yourself.

Forgive someone today,
just as you would want
Allāh to forgive you!

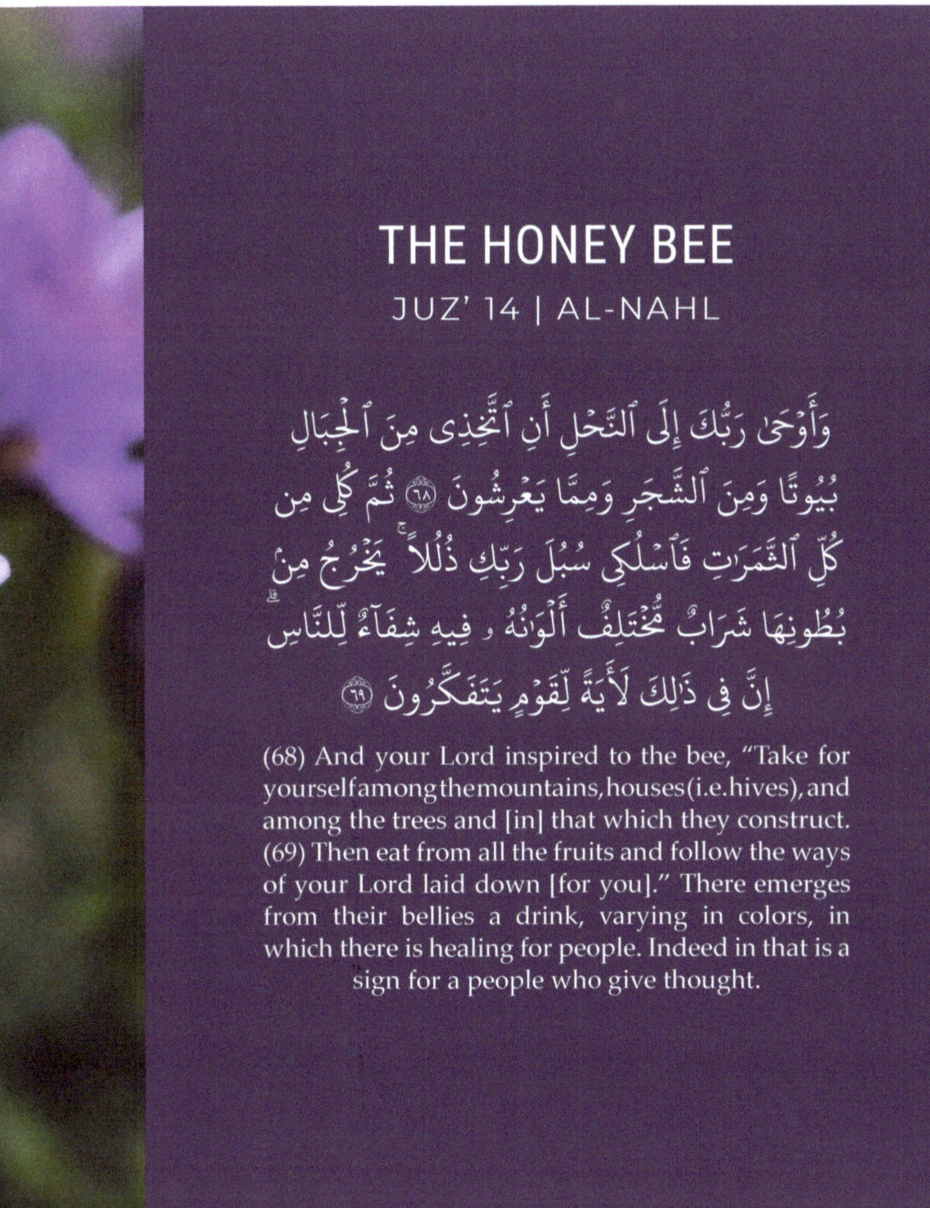

THE HONEY BEE

JUZ' 14 | AL-NAHL

وَأَوْحَىٰ رَبُّكَ إِلَى ٱلنَّحْلِ أَنِ ٱتَّخِذِى مِنَ ٱلْجِبَالِ بُيُوتًا وَمِنَ ٱلشَّجَرِ وَمِمَّا يَعْرِشُونَ ۝ ثُمَّ كُلِى مِن كُلِّ ٱلثَّمَرَٰتِ فَٱسْلُكِى سُبُلَ رَبِّكِ ذُلُلاً ۚ يَخْرُجُ مِن بُطُونِهَا شَرَابٌ مُّخْتَلِفٌ أَلْوَٰنُهُ ۥ فِيهِ شِفَآءٌ لِّلنَّاسِ ۗ إِنَّ فِى ذَٰلِكَ لَأَيَةً لِّقَوْمٍ يَتَفَكَّرُونَ ۝

(68) And your Lord inspired to the bee, "Take for yourself among the mountains, houses (i.e. hives), and among the trees and [in] that which they construct. (69) Then eat from all the fruits and follow the ways of your Lord laid down [for you]." There emerges from their bellies a drink, varying in colors, in which there is healing for people. Indeed in that is a sign for a people who give thought.

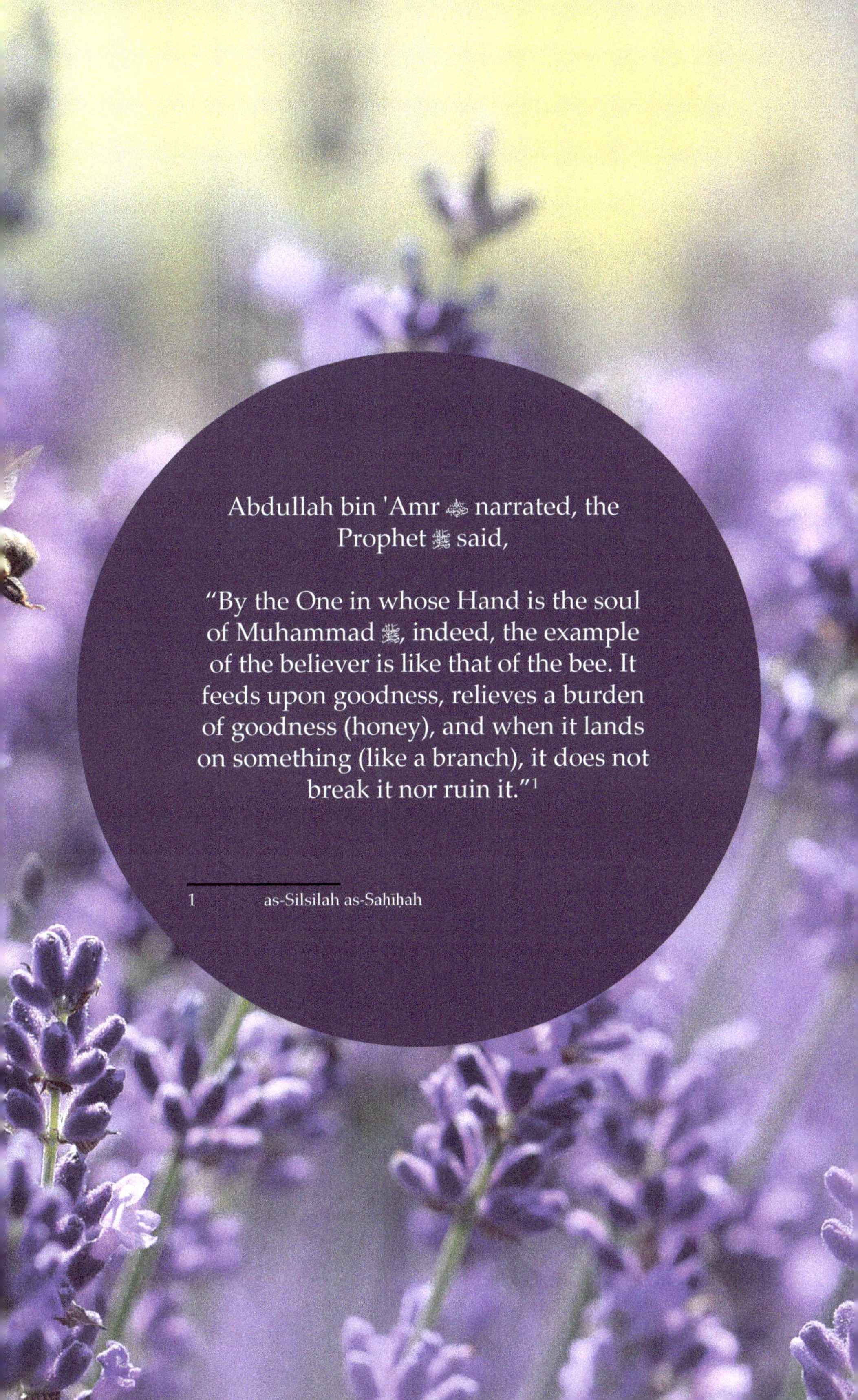

Abdullah bin 'Amr ﷺ narrated, the Prophet ﷺ said,

"By the One in whose Hand is the soul of Muhammad ﷺ, indeed, the example of the believer is like that of the bee. It feeds upon goodness, relieves a burden of goodness (honey), and when it lands on something (like a branch), it does not break it nor ruin it."[1]

[1]   as-Silsilah as-Saḥīḥah

PARENTS

وَقَضَىٰ رَبُّكَ أَلَّا تَعْبُدُوٓا۟ إِلَّآ إِيَّاهُ وَبِٱلْوَٰلِدَيْنِ إِحْسَٰنًا إِمَّا يَبْلُغَنَّ عِندَكَ ٱلْكِبَرَ أَحَدُهُمَآ أَوْ كِلَاهُمَا فَلَا تَقُل لَّهُمَآ أُفٍّ وَلَا تَنْهَرْهُمَا وَقُل لَّهُمَا قَوْلًا كَرِيمًا ۝ وَٱخْفِضْ لَهُمَا جَنَاحَ ٱلذُّلِّ مِنَ ٱلرَّحْمَةِ وَقُل رَّبِّ ٱرْحَمْهُمَا كَمَا رَبَّيَانِى صَغِيرًا ۝

(23) And your Lord has decreed that you not worship except Him, and to parents, good treatment. Whether one or both of them reach old age [while] with you, say not to them [so much as], "uff", and do not repel them but speak to them a noble word. (24) And lower to them the wing of humility out of mercy and say, "My Lord, have mercy upon them as they brought me up [when I was] small."

After the right of Allāh, the next greatest right is that of one's parents out of all people. They deserve nothing less than good treatment. And in this *āyah*, the attainment of old age is specially mentioned because at that age parents become weak and frail, and the child becomes strong and able, and since the ways of the young and elderly differ, this may lead to conflicts.

Hence, children are commanded here to humble themselves before their parents and treat them with utmost kindness, respect and appreciation.

Good conduct towards parents especially the mother

A man came to the Prophet ﷺ and asked, "O Messenger of Allāh, who among people is most deserving of my good company?" He said, "Your mother." He said, "Then who?" He said, "Then your mother." He said, "Then who?" He said, "Then your mother." He said, "Then who?" He said, "Then your father."[1]

Good treatment to parents in old age takes one to jannah

The Prophet ﷺ said, "He is doomed, he is doomed, he is doomed, the man whose parents, one or both of them, reach old age while he is alive and he does not enter Paradise."[2]

---

1   Saḥīḥ al-Bukhārī, Book 78 Hadith 2
2   Musnad Aḥmed

Making parents cry is a major sin

'Abdullah ibn 'Amr ﷺ said, "A man came to the Prophet ﷺ and made a pledge to him that he would do *hijrah* (migration). He left his parents who were in tears. The Prophet ﷺ said, 'Go back to them and make them smile as you made them weep.'"[1]

Ibn 'Umar ﷺ said, "Making parents weep is part of disobedience and one of the major wrong actions."

Our respect for our parents should be impeccable in every situation to the best of our ability

Abu Hurairah ﷺ saw two men and said to one of them, "Who is this man in relation to you?" "He is my father," he replied. He said, "Do not call him by his own name nor walk in front of him nor sit down before him."[2]

Make *du'ā* for them

Abu Hurairah ﷺ said, "The dead person is raised a degree after his death. He said, 'My Lord, how is this?' He was told, 'Your child seeking forgiveness for you.'"[3]

1   al-Adab al-Mufrad, Book 1 Hadith 31
2   al-Adab al-Mufrad, Book 1 Hadith 44
3   al-Adab al-Mufrad, Book 1 Hadith 36

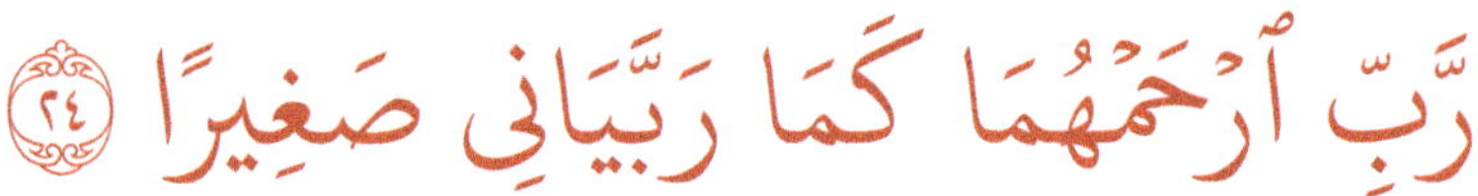

رَّبِّ ٱرْحَمْهُمَا كَمَا رَبَّيَانِي صَغِيرًا ۞

"My Lord, have mercy upon them as they
brought me up [when I was] small."
[al-Isrā':24]

RELIEF

JUZ' 16 | MARYAM

كهيعص ﴿١﴾ ذِكْرُ رَحْمَتِ رَبِّكَ عَبْدَهُ زَكَرِيَّآ ﴿٢﴾ إِذْ نَادَىٰ رَبَّهُۥ نِدَآءً خَفِيًّا ﴿٣﴾ قَالَ رَبِّ إِنِّى وَهَنَ ٱلْعَظْمُ مِنِّى وَٱشْتَعَلَ ٱلرَّأْسُ شَيْبًا وَلَمْ أَكُنۢ بِدُعَآئِكَ رَبِّ شَقِيًّا ﴿٤﴾

(1) Kaf, Ha, Ya, 'Ayn, Sad. (2) [This is] a mention of the mercy of your Lord to His servant Zakariyya (3) When he called to his Lord a private supplication. (4) He said, "My Lord, indeed my bones have weakened, and my head has filled with white, and never have I been in my supplication to You, my Lord, unhappy (i.e. disappointed)."

From these *āyāt*, we learn not only the *du'ā* of Zakariyya, but also how to make *du'ā*. Zakariyya converted his *du'ā* into a heartfelt conversation with his Lord, a *du'ā* in which he showed utmost humility, in which he listed his weaknesses before Allāh and at the same time demonstrated absolute conviction!

Continue to make *du'ā* and never give up. Be hopeful for a response from Allāh. It is in your greatest need that you will find the greatest relief from Allāh when you are hopeful.

The night is darkest just before dawn; relief is around the corner, the help of Allāh is near, so keep turning to Him and ask Him. Never despair of His mercy and never think that what you are asking for is impossible because for Allāh, nothing is impossible!

Every single sincere *du'ā* is guaranteed a response from Allāh in one of three ways:

The Prophet ﷺ said, "No Muslim supplicates to Allāh with a *du'ā* that does not involve sin or cutting the relations of the womb, but Allāh will grant him one of the three things. He will either hasten the response to his supplication (he is given exactly what he wants), save it for him until the Hereafter, or would turn an equivalent amount of evil away from him." They (the Saḥāba) said, "In that case we will ask for more!" He said, "Allāh has even more!"[1]

---

1 Riyad as-Salihin, Book 16 Hadith 37

SUPPLICATION OF THE DISTRESSED
JUZ' 17 | AL-ANBIYĀ

وَذَا ٱلنُّونِ إِذ ذَّهَبَ مُغَـٰضِبًا فَظَنَّ أَن لَّن نَّقْدِرَ
عَلَيْهِ فَنَادَىٰ فِى ٱلظُّلُمَـٰتِ أَن لَّآ إِلَـٰهَ إِلَّآ أَنتَ
سُبْحَـٰنَكَ إِنِّى كُنتُ مِنَ ٱلظَّـٰلِمِينَ ۝ فَٱسْتَجَبْنَا لَهُۥ
وَنَجَّيْنَـٰهُ مِنَ ٱلْغَمِّ ۚ وَكَذَٰلِكَ نُـۨجِى ٱلْمُؤْمِنِينَ ۝

(87) And [mention] the man of the fish, when he (Yunus) went off in anger and thought that We would not decree [anything] upon him. And he called out within the darknesses, "There is no deity except You; exalted are You. Indeed, I have been of the wrong-doers." (88) So We responded to him and saved him from the distress. And thus do We save the believers.

When the distressed person sincerely calls upon Allāh, the doors of the heaven open up for his *du'ā* and his *du'ā* is not turned away.

The Messenger of Allāh ﷺ said, "The supplication of Dhun-Nūn (Prophet Yūnus ﷺ) when he supplicated, while in the belly of the whale was:

لَّآ إِلَـٰهَ إِلَّآ أَنتَ سُبْحَـٰنَكَ إِنِّى كُنتُ مِنَ ٱلظَّـٰلِمِين

'There is no deity except You; exalted are You. Indeed, I have been of the wrongdoers.'

So indeed, no Muslim supplicates with it for anything, ever, except Allāh responds to him."[1]

Some other supplications at the time of distress:

Asma' bint Umays ﷺ narrated, "The Messenger of Allāh ﷺ said to me, 'Shall I not teach you words which you utter in distress (*karb*)? These are:

اللَّهُ اللَّهُ رَبِّي لاَ أُشْرِكُ بِهِ شَيْئًا

Allāh, Allāh is my Lord, I do not associate anything as partner with Him.'"[2]

Ibn 'Abbas ﷺ narrated that the Prophet ﷺ used to supplicate during the *karb* (in these words):

لاَ إِلَهَ إِلَّا اللَّهُ الْعَظِيمُ الْحَلِيمُ لاَ إِلَهَ إِلَّا اللَّهُ رَبُّ الْعَرْشِ الْعَظِيمِ لاَ إِلَهَ إِلَّا اللَّهُ

رَبُّ السَّمَاوَاتِ وَرَبُّ الأَرْضِ وَرَبُّ الْعَرْشِ الْكَرِيمِ

"There is no god but Allāh, the Most Great, the Most Forbearing, there is no god but Allāh, the Lord of the Magnificent Throne, There is no god but Allāh, the Lord of the Heavens and the earth, the Lord of the Noble Throne."[3]

---

1   Jami' at-Tirmidhī, Book 48 Hadith 136
2   Sunan Abu Dawūd, Book 8 Hadith 110
3   Mishkat al-Masabih, Book 9 Hadith 187

THE PATH TO SUCCESS
JUZ' 18 | AL-MU'MINŪN

قَدْ أَفْلَحَ ٱلْمُؤْمِنُونَ ۝ ٱلَّذِينَ هُمْ فِى صَلَاتِهِمْ خَٰشِعُونَ ۝ وَٱلَّذِينَ هُمْ عَنِ ٱللَّغْوِ مُعْرِضُونَ ۝ وَٱلَّذِينَ هُمْ لِلزَّكَوٰةِ فَٰعِلُونَ ۝ وَٱلَّذِينَ هُمْ لِفُرُوجِهِمْ حَٰفِظُونَ ۝ إِلَّا عَلَىٰ أَزْوَٰجِهِمْ أَوْ مَا مَلَكَتْ أَيْمَٰنُهُمْ فَإِنَّهُمْ غَيْرُ مَلُومِينَ ۝ فَمَنِ ٱبْتَغَىٰ وَرَآءَ ذَٰلِكَ فَأُوْلَٰئِكَ هُمُ ٱلْعَادُونَ ۝ وَٱلَّذِينَ هُمْ لِأَمَٰنَٰتِهِمْ وَعَهْدِهِمْ رَٰعُونَ ۝ وَٱلَّذِينَ هُمْ عَلَىٰ صَلَوَٰتِهِمْ يُحَافِظُونَ ۝ أُوْلَٰئِكَ هُمُ ٱلْوَٰرِثُونَ ۝ ٱلَّذِينَ يَرِثُونَ ٱلْفِرْدَوْسَ هُمْ فِيهَا خَٰلِدُونَ ۝

(1) Certainly will the believers have succeeded: (2) They who are during their prayer humbly submissive, (3) And they who turn away from ill speech, (4) And they who are observant of zakah, (5) And they who guard their private parts, (6) Except from their wives or those their right hands possess, for indeed, they will not be blamed - (7) But whoever seeks beyond that, then those are the transgressors - (8) And they who are to their trusts and their promises attentive, (9) And they who carefully maintain their prayers - (10) Those are the inheritors, (11) Who will inherit al-Firdaws. They will abide therein eternally.

In these *āyāt*, Allāh has clearly outlined the way to success. The one who adopts this way will attain eternal success and–such happiness–for which there will be no decline.

Things to do to achieve this success:

• Develop *Khushū'* (humility and submissiveness) in *Salāh*.

• Guard the tongue by avoiding ill speech.

• Observe *Zakāt* (almsgiving).

• Guard modesty and chastity.

• Be trustworthy and honest by rendering the trust and fulfilling promises.

• Guard the prayer by taking care of its prerequisites, conditions, and pillars.

The Reward for observing these noble deeds is Al-Firdaws!

The Messenger of Allāh ﷺ said, "Paradise has one hundred levels and between each two levels is a distance like that between the heavens and earth. *Al-Firdaws* is its highest level, from which four rivers of Paradise flow and above which is the Throne. When you ask from Allāh, ask for *Al-Firdaws*."[1]

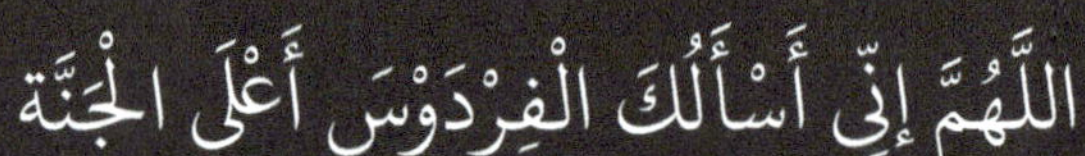

اللَّهُمَّ إِنِّي أَسْأَلُكَ الْفِرْدَوْسَ أَعْلَى الْجَنَّة

---

1 Sunan Ibn Majah, Book 37 Hadith 232

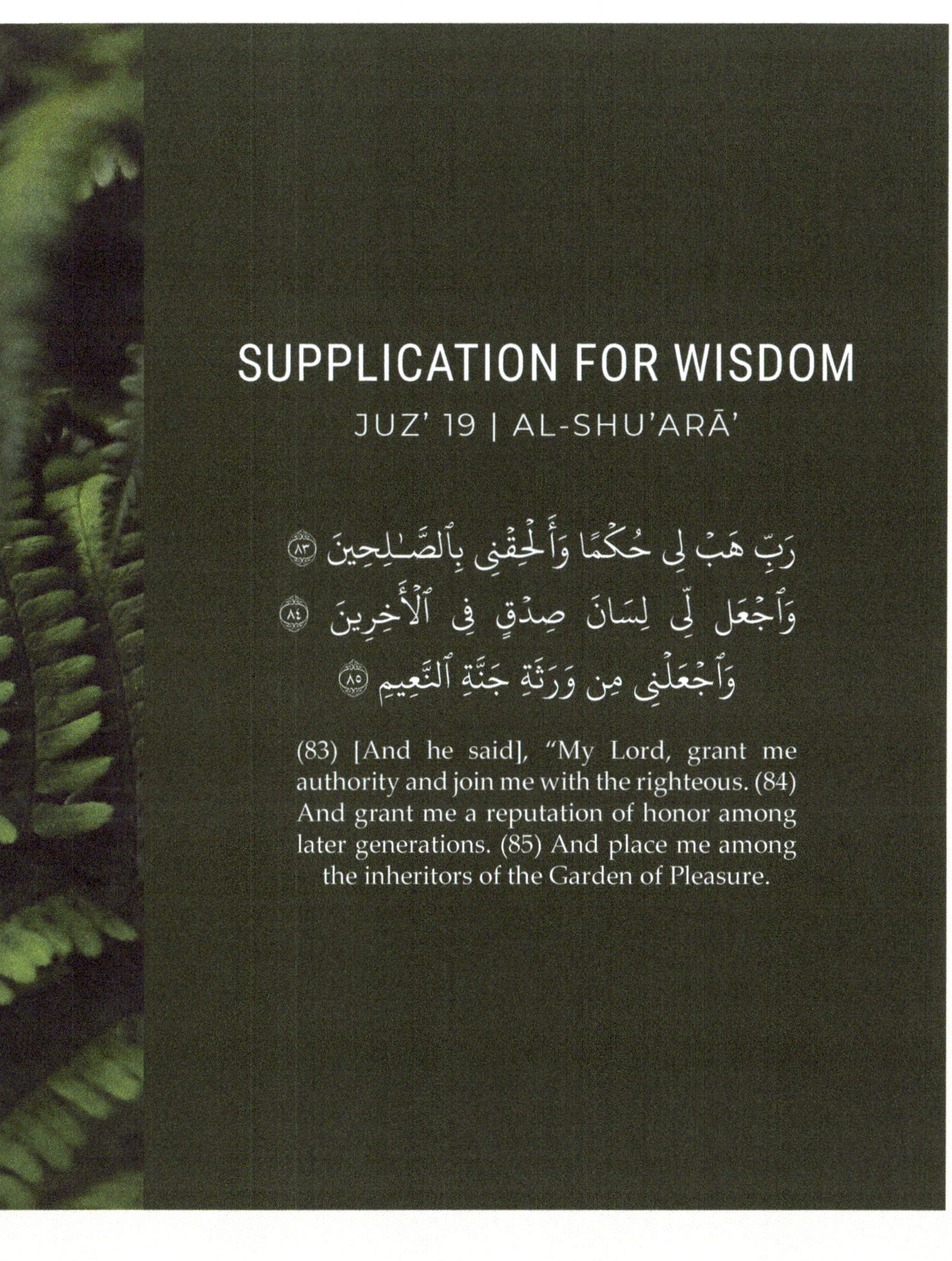

SUPPLICATION FOR WISDOM
JUZ' 19 | AL-SHU'ARĀ'

رَبِّ هَبْ لِى حُكْمًا وَأَلْحِقْنِى بِالصَّـٰلِحِينَ ۝
وَٱجْعَل لِّى لِسَانَ صِدْقٍ فِى ٱلْأَخِرِينَ ۝
وَٱجْعَلْنِى مِن وَرَثَةِ جَنَّةِ ٱلنَّعِيمِ ۝

(83) [And he said], "My Lord, grant me authority and join me with the righteous. (84) And grant me a reputation of honor among later generations. (85) And place me among the inheritors of the Garden of Pleasure.

Ask Allāh for:

1. Wisdom, sound judgment, understanding of the Religion

The Prophet ﷺ said, "When Allāh wishes good for someone, He gives him understanding of the Religion."[1]

2. Righteous company

Whoever a person loves, he is going to be with them:

Anas ؓ narrated, "A man asked the Prophet ﷺ about the Hour saying, 'When will the Hour be?' The Prophet ﷺ said, 'What have you prepared for it?' The man said, 'Nothing, except that I love Allāh and His Messenger.' The Prophet ﷺ said, 'You will be with those whom you love.'" Anas ؓ said, "We had never been so happy as we were on hearing that saying of the Prophet ﷺ (i.e., 'You will be with those whom you love.') Therefore, I love the Prophet ﷺ, Abu Bakr and 'Umar, and I hope that I will be with them because of my love for them though my deeds are not similar to theirs."[2]

SubḥanAllāh! Even though our actions are not as great, we love the righteous, we love the Prophets, the companions and hope and pray that we will be with them.

3. *Lisāna Sidqin*

A reputation of honor, a good and truthful mention, that we leave behind a good legacy so that we become an example to be followed.

4. Paradise

Home of everlasting bliss and pleasure!

---

1   Riyad as-Salihin, Book 12 Hadith 1
2   Saḥīh al-Bukhārī, Book 62 Hadith 38

FULFILLED NEEDS

JUZ' 20 | AL-QASAS

فَفَسَقَىٰ لَهُمَا ثُمَّ تَوَلَّىٰ إِلَى ٱلظِّلِّ فَقَالَ رَبِّ إِنِّى لِمَآ أَنزَلْتَ إِلَىَّ مِنْ خَيْرٍ فَقِيرٌ ۝

(24) So he watered [their flocks] for them; then he went back to the shade and said, "My Lord, indeed I am, for whatever good You would send down to me, in need."

Mūsa ﷺ expressed his absolute and total dependency on Allāh when he made this *du'ā* at a time when the future seemed so uncertain. Almost immediately his *du'ā* was answered. How did this happen; that his *du'ā* was answered right away and his difficulty resolved? Musa resolved someone else's difficulty first!

As mentioned at the beginning of the *āyah*, he unconditionally helpedanotherwithout expecting anything in return. Hence, when he made *du'ā* to Allāh for his own needs, soon the help of Allāh came.

Abu Hurairah ﷺ narrated that the Prophet ﷺ said, "Whoever removes a worldly grief from a believer, Allāh will remove from him one of the griefs of the Day of Resurrection. And whoever alleviates the need of a needy person, Allāh will alleviate his needs in this world and the Hereafter. Whoever shields [or hides the faults of] a Muslim, Allāh will shield him in this world and the Hereafter. And Allāh will help His slave so long as he helps his brother."[1]

The Prophet ﷺ said, "Of the most virtuous of deeds is to put a smile on the face of a believer, pay off his debt, fulfill some need of his, or remove some hardship from him."[2]

So if we would want our problems to be resolved, hardships to be lightened, difficulties to be removed, then we should do the same for others. Do good to others, good will be done to you; forgive others, you will be forgiven; have mercy upon others, you will be shown mercy!

It is the promise of Allāh:

$$إِنَّ اللَّهَ لَا يُضِيعُ أَجْرَ ٱلْمُحْسِنِينَ$$

Indeed, Allāh does not allow to be lost the reward of the doers of good. [Al-Tawbah:120]

---

1   40 Hadith of Nawawi, Hadith 36
2   as-Silsilah as-Saḥīḥah

Do good to others,
and good will be done to you.
It is the promise of Allāh!

THE LIFE OF EVERLASTING BLISS
JUZ' 21 | AL-'ANKABŪT

وَمَا هَـٰذِهِ ٱلْحَيَوٰةُ ٱلدُّنْيَآ إِلَّا لَهْوٌ وَلَعِبٌ وَإِنَّ ٱلدَّارَ ٱلْأَخِرَةَ لَهِىَ ٱلْحَيَوَانُ لَوْ كَانُوا۟ يَعْلَمُونَ ۝

(64) And this worldly life is not but diversion and amusement. And indeed, the home of the Hereafter-that is the [eternal] life, if only they knew.

Every pleasure of this world comes with some pain because the *Dunyā* (world) is imperfect and temporary. Whereas, the pleasure of the Hereafter is the real pleasure, as the *Ākhirah* (hereafter) is perfect and eternal. It is not tainted by any imperfection, deficiency, sadness, or decline.

The Prophet ﷺ said, "An announcer (in Paradise) would announce, 'Indeed, there is for you (everlasting) health and you shall never fall sick, you will live (forever) and never die, you will forever remain young and never grow old, and you will always live in affluence and never become destitute, as the words of Allāh, the Exalted and Glorious, are:

$$وَنُودُوا أَن تِلْكُمُ الْجَنَّةُ أُورِثْتُمُوهَا بِمَا كُنتُمْ تَعْمَلُونَ$$

'And they will be called, 'This is Paradise, which you have been made to inherit for what you used to do.'' (al-A'rāf:43)"[1]

The life of the Hereafter will be perfect in every way!

The Prophet ﷺ was asked, 'O Messenger of Allāh, do the people of Paradise sleep?' The Prophet ﷺ said, 'Sleep is the sister of death, and the people of Paradise do not sleep.'"[2]

In this world, when you are having the time of your life, the last thing you want to do is sleep, but alas, sleep overcomes you. In Paradise, however, the dwellers will enjoy eternal pleasure and happiness! There will be no tiredness, fatigue, nor boredom in Jannah. That life is the eternal life! So we must tire ourselves in worship and good deeds here so that we can enjoy there; we must work hard here so that we can rest there.

May Allāh allow us to use our blessings and abilities to earn His Pleasure.

---

1   Ṣaḥīḥ Muslim, Book 53 Hadith 26
2   al-Mu'jam al-Awsat

THE UPPER HAND

JUZ' 22 | SABA

قُل إِنَّ رَبِّي يَبْسُطُ ٱلرِّزْقَ لِمَن يَشَآءُ مِنْ عِبَادِهِۦ وَيَقْدِرُ لَهُۥ ۚ وَمَآ أَنفَقْتُم مِّن شَىْءٍ فَهُوَ يُخْلِفُهُۥ ۖ وَهُوَ خَيْرُ ٱلرَّٰزِقِينَ ﴿٣٩﴾

(39) Say, "Indeed, my Lord extends provision for whom He wills of His servants and restricts [it] for him. But whatever thing you spend [in His cause] - He will compensate it; and He is the best of providers."

Subḥan Allāh! Whatever you spend in Allāh's way will never ever be lost! Rather, you will definitely be compensated for it. When one thing goes, another comes in its place. Allāh will recompense you with the best return here in this world and also in the Hereafter.

The Prophet ﷺ said, "Allāh said: 'Spend, O son of Adam, and I shall spend on you.'"[1]

Allāh gives, gives and keeps giving!

The Prophet ﷺ said, "The right Hand of Allāh is full and it is not lessened by the continuous spending night and day. Have you seen what He has spent since He created the heavens and the earth? Yet all that has not decreased what is in His Right Hand."[2]

Give from what Allāh has given even if it is something as small as a date-fruit!

The Prophet ﷺ said, "None gives charity from what is good, for Allāh only accepts what is good, but that the Most Merciful takes it with His right Hand. Even if it is a date, it is nurtured in the Hand of the Most Merciful until it becomes greater than a mountain, just as one of you nurtures his young horse or camel."[3]

Giving is a means of increase in blessings

The Prophet ﷺ said, "Allāh gives special blessings to some of His servants in order to benefit His creation through them. If he spends, then his blessings remain safe, and if he withholds then Allāh takes it away from him and gives to others."[4]

---

1 Saḥīḥ al-Bukhārī, Book 69 Hadith 2
2 Saḥīḥ al-Bukhari, Book 97 Hadith 47
3 Jami' at-Tirmidhi, Book 7 Hadith 45
4 as-Silsilah as-Saḥīḥah

Give and do not fear poverty

The Prophet ﷺ said to Bilal ؓ, "Spend O Bilal, and fear not poverty from the Owner of the Throne."[5]

Give, especially in the month of Ramadan

Ibn Abbas ؓ said, "The Prophet ﷺ was the most generous of all the people, and he used to become more generous in Ramadān when Jibrīl met him. Jibrīl used to meet him every night during Ramadān to revise the Qur'ān with him. Allāh's Messenger ﷺ then used to be more generous than the fast wind."[6]

May Allāh enable us to benefit others through the blessings He has given us.

---

5   Mishkat al-Masabih, Book 6 Hadith 112
6   Saḥīḥ al-Bukhārī, Book 61 Hadith 112

THE ROWS OF THE ANGELS
JUZ' 23 | AL-SĀFFĀT

وَٱلصَّٰفَّٰتِ صَفًّا ۝ فَٱلزَّٰجِرَٰتِ زَجْرًا ۝ فَٱلتَّٰلِيَٰتِ ذِكْرًا ۝ إِنَّ إِلَٰهَكُمْ لَوَٰحِدٌ ۝ رَّبُّ ٱلسَّمَٰوَٰتِ وَٱلْأَرْضِ وَمَا بَيْنَهُمَا وَرَبُّ ٱلْمَشَٰرِقِ ۝

(1) By those [angels] lined up in rows (2) And those who drive [the clouds] (3) And those who recite the message, (4) Indeed, your God is One, (5) Lord of the heavens and the earth and that between them and Lord of the sunrises.

Angels demonstrate impeccable obedience and submission to Allāh. They are ever ready to implement the commands of Allāh and do as they are told. They are extremely disciplined and organized, forming rows and in unison obey their Lord. They arrange themselves in perfect rows out of utmost respect for the One before whom they stand. This is how they worship and also how they receive commands from their Lord.

The rows of the angels

The Prophet ﷺ said, "Will you not form rows as the angels form rows in the presence of their Lord?" We said, "How do the angels form rows in the presence of their Lord?" He said, "They complete the first rows and keep close together in the row (leaving no gaps)."[1]

A special favour

The Prophet ﷺ said, "We have been favoured over the rest of mankind in three ways: our rows have been made like the rows of the angels (completely straight rows); the entire earth has been made a *Masjid* (mosque) for us; and its soil has been made a means of purification for us if we cannot find water."[2]

Forming straight rows is a part of establishing *Salāh*

The Prophet ﷺ said, "Establish straight rows in prayer, for the straightening of rows is among those things which make your prayer good and perfect."[3]

---

1   Sunan an-Nasa'i, Book 10 Hadith 40
2   Ṣaḥīḥ Muslim
3   Riyad as-Salihin, Book 8 Hadith 97

A means of receiving Allāh's Mercy

The Prophet ﷺ said, "Keep your rows straight for your rows resemble those of the angels. Join the shoulders and fill the gaps between yourselves, be gentle and soft in your brothers' hands and do not leave gaps for *shaitān*. He who connects a row, Allāh will connect him (with His mercy), and he who breaks a row, Allāh will cut him off (from His mercy)."[4]

A means of strength and unity, and a way of earning Allāh's Pleasure

Al-Bara' ibn Azib ﷺ narrated, "The Messenger of Allāh ﷺ used to pass through the row from one side to the other; he used to set our chests and shoulders in order, and say, 'Do not be irregular (differ) or else your hearts will differ.' And he would say, 'Indeed, Allāh and His angels send blessings upon those who are in the first rows.'"[5]

4   Musnad Aḥmad
5   Sunan Abu Dawūd, Book 2 Hadith 274

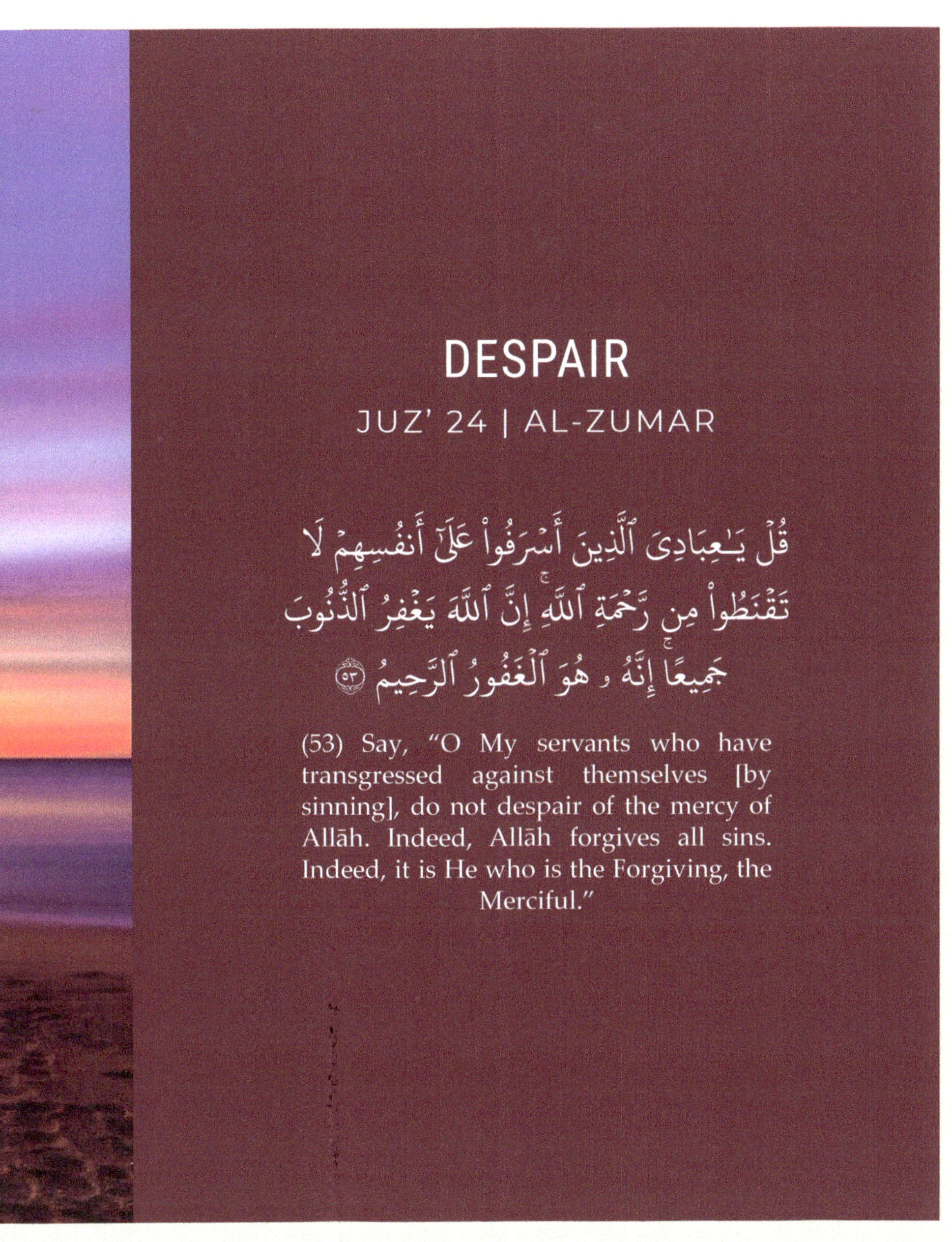

DESPAIR
JUZ' 24 | AL-ZUMAR

قُلْ يَٰعِبَادِيَ ٱلَّذِينَ أَسْرَفُواْ عَلَىٰٓ أَنفُسِهِمْ لَا تَقْنَطُواْ مِن رَّحْمَةِ ٱللَّهِ إِنَّ ٱللَّهَ يَغْفِرُ ٱلذُّنُوبَ جَمِيعًا إِنَّهُۥ وَهُوَ ٱلْغَفُورُ ٱلرَّحِيمُ ۝

(53) Say, "O My servants who have transgressed against themselves [by sinning], do not despair of the mercy of Allāh. Indeed, Allāh forgives all sins. Indeed, it is He who is the Forgiving, the Merciful."

Allāh addresses all of humanity very lovingly and compassionately, specifically those who have transgressed against themselves by sinning. It is an invitation to not despair, to have hope in Allāh's Mercy and turn to Him in repentance.

Never ever think that you are unforgivable no matter how many mistakes you have made, how bad your past is or how embarrassed you feel about it. Because Allāh forgives all sins regardless of their magnitude and great numbers! So long as you leave the sin and turn back to Him, raise your hands and pray to Him.

The Messenger of Allāh ﷺ said, "Allāh the Almighty has said, 'O Son of Adam, as long as you invoke Me and ask of Me, I shall forgive you for what you have done, and I shall not mind. O Son of Adam, were your sins to reach the clouds of the sky and you then asked forgiveness from Me, I would forgive you. O Son of Adam, were you to come to Me with sins nearly as great as the Earth, and were you then to face Me, ascribing no partner to Me, I would bring you forgiveness nearly as great as it [too].'"[1]

Allāh loves to forgive (*tuḥibbul-'Afw*). One of Allāh's Names is *al-Ghaffār* (The One Who Forgives the Most), and *al-Ghafūr* (The One Who Forgives); the *maghfirah* (forgiveness) from Allāh is a sign of His Love and Mercy towards His creation. Even if the sins are the size of a mountain, or the amount of foam on the sea, Allāh forgives them when His servant turns to Him seeking forgiveness.

May Allāh forgive us and have mercy on us.

ANGER MANAGEMENT
JUZ' 25 | AL-SHŪRĀ

فَفَمَآ أُوتِيتُم مِّن شَىْءٍ فَمَتَٰعُ ٱلْحَيَوٰةِ ٱلدُّنْيَا وَمَا عِندَ ٱللَّهِ خَيْرٌ وَأَبْقَىٰ لِلَّذِينَ ءَامَنُوا۟ وَعَلَىٰ رَبِّهِمْ يَتَوَكَّلُونَ ۞ وَٱلَّذِينَ يَجْتَنِبُونَ كَبَٰٓئِرَ ٱلْإِثْمِ وَٱلْفَوَٰحِشَ وَإِذَا مَا غَضِبُوا۟ هُمْ يَغْفِرُونَ ۞

(36) So whatever thing you have been given - it is but [for] enjoyment of the worldly life. But what is with Allāh is better and more lasting for those who have believed and upon their Lord rely (37) And those who avoid the major sins and immoralities, and when they are angry, they forgive.

Every single person experiences some level of anger, be it a little or a lot, and this is something very natural. But what is important is to know how to channel it properly, how to let go and forgive, how to not persist and act on it.

When we express our anger passively or aggressively, we are not only hurting the other, but are also hurting ourselves. Anger is one letter short of danger, it is destructive! This is why it is so important that we control our anger and not let it control us.

Controlling anger leads to Paradise

The Prophet ﷺ said, "Do not get angry, and Paradise will be yours."[1]

Do not be angry with others, Allāh will not be angry with you

Abdullah ibn Amr ؓ asked the Prophet ﷺ "What will distance me from Allāh's anger?" The Prophet ﷺ said, "Do not get angry!"[2]

SubḥanAllāh, when you let go and forgive Allāh's creation, Allāh will forgive you! This is why, learn to forgive and let go, join and not cut off, mend and not break, and make a lot of *du'ā* to Allāh, seeking His help and assistance.

---

1   Saḥīḥ al-Jāmi al-Saghīr 7374
2   Musnad Aḥmed 6597

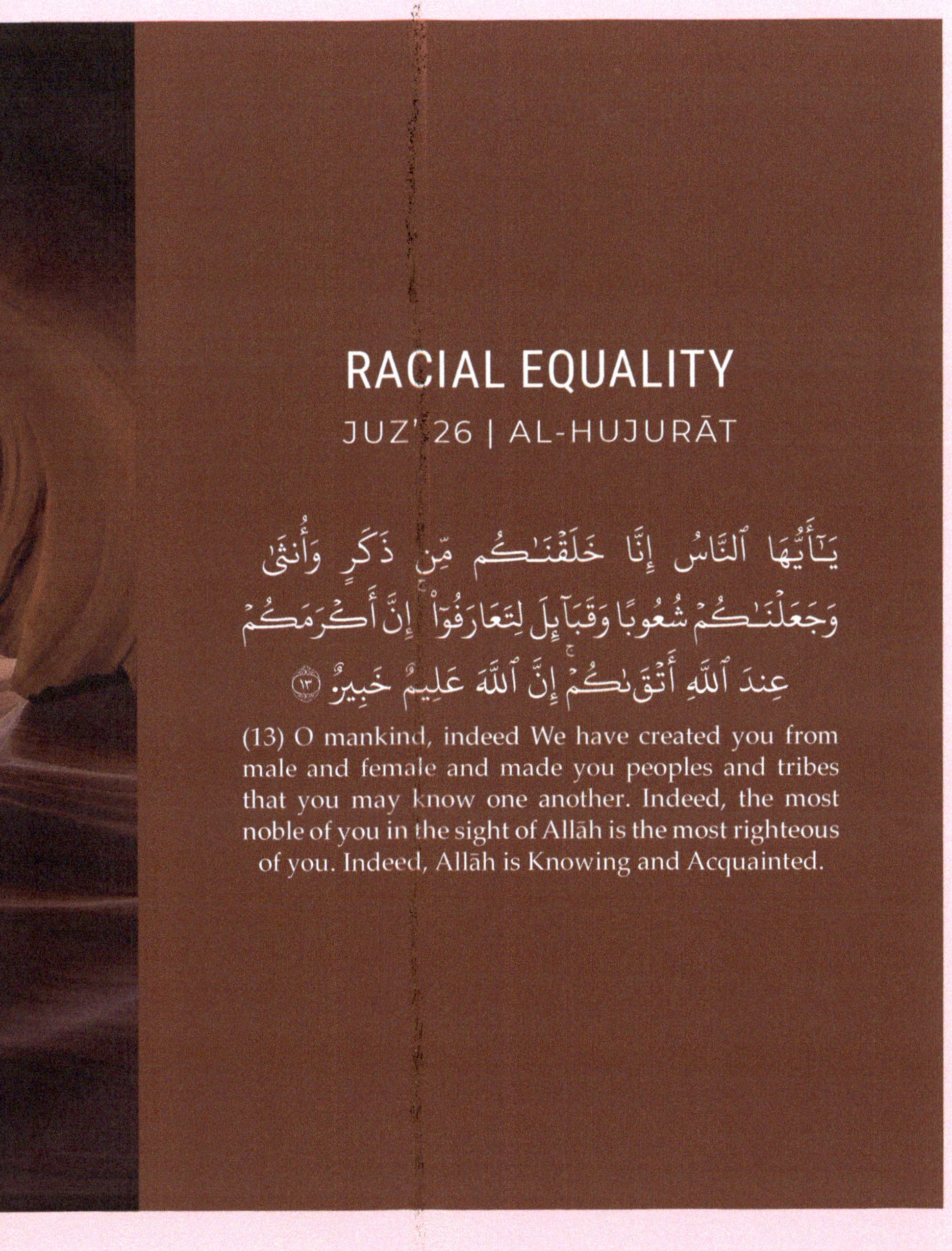

RACIAL EQUALITY
JUZ' 26 | AL-HUJURĀT

يَـٰٓأَيُّهَا ٱلنَّاسُ إِنَّا خَلَقْنَـٰكُم مِّن ذَكَرٍ وَأُنثَىٰ وَجَعَلْنَـٰكُمْ شُعُوبًا وَقَبَآئِلَ لِتَعَارَفُوٓا۟ إِنَّ أَكْرَمَكُمْ عِندَ ٱللَّهِ أَتْقَىٰكُمْ إِنَّ ٱللَّهَ عَلِيمٌ خَبِيرٌ ۝

(13) O mankind, indeed We have created you from male and female and made you peoples and tribes that you may know one another. Indeed, the most noble of you in the sight of Allāh is the most righteous of you. Indeed, Allāh is Knowing and Acquainted.

This *āyah* establishes racial equality.

All people are related to one another, tracing their lineage back to the same mother and father. We are all the children of Adam, therefore, none is superior to the other in terms of lineage. Why then are there different races and ancestries? The purpose is identification - so that people recognise each other and also learn from each other. Ethnic diversity is a means of enrichment. If everyone were the same, then there would be no variety, no diversity in languages, cultures or cuisines! There is beauty and purpose in this variation, which is why one should never consider himself better than others based on his race and ancestry.

Nobility and honour in the sight of Allāh is not by what you were born with, but it is by what you do. It is not by how you look, but by how you look at others. It is not by your ascribed characteristics of family, race, ethnicity, colour, height, and appearance, but it is by your achieved characteristics of piety and righteousness. Honour and distinction is by righteousness and moral quality, not by birth, race or nationality.

The Prophet ﷺ said at the farewell pilgrimage, "O people, your Lord is one and your father Adam is one. There is no favour of an Arab over a non-Arab, nor a non-Arab over an Arab, and neither white skin over black skin, nor black skin over white skin, except by righteousness. Have I not delivered the message?"[1]

Therefore, we should attain distinction near Allāh by excelling in piety and good deeds in the heart and its demonstration in actions.

---

1   Musnad Aḥmed 23489

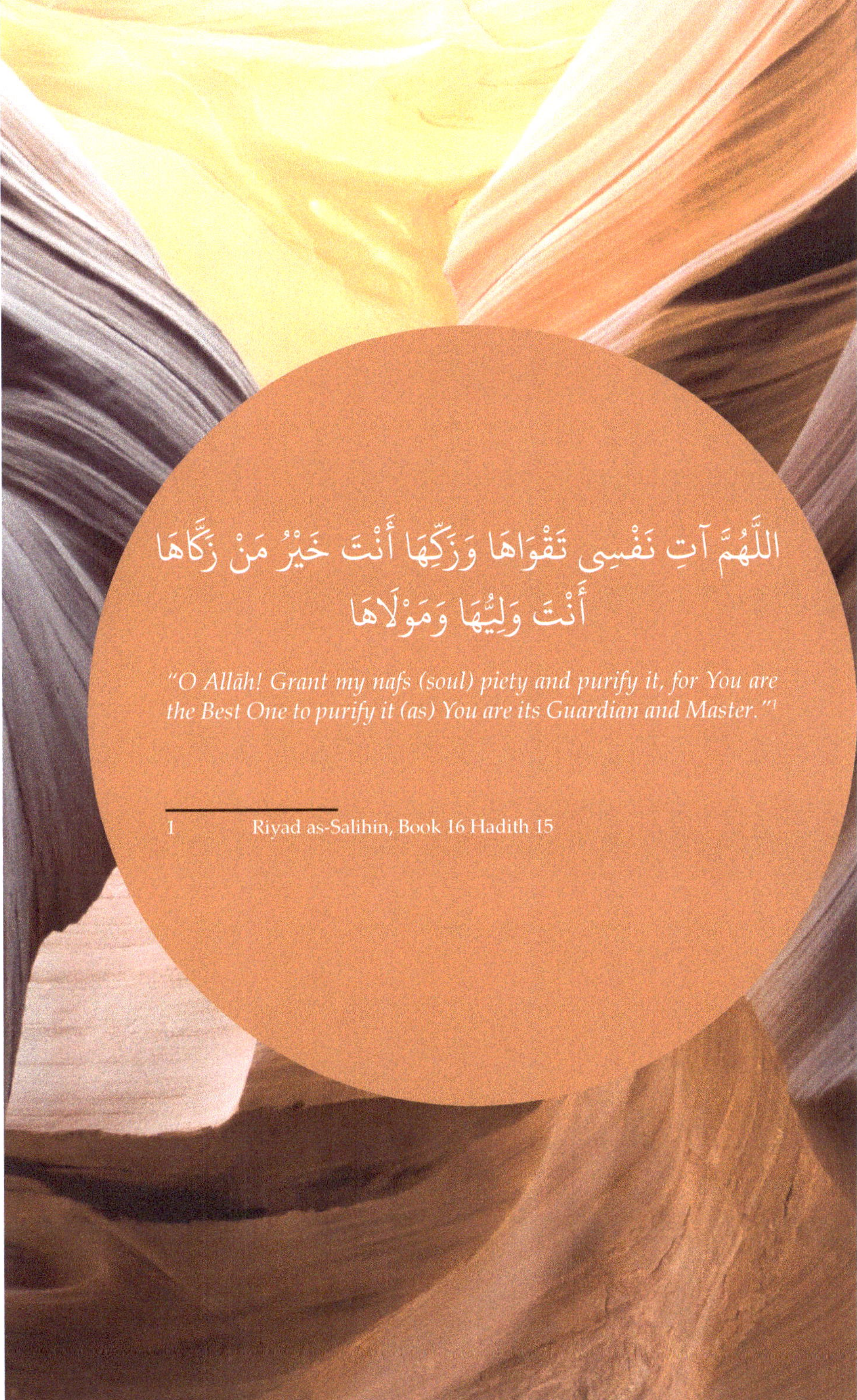

"O Allāh! Grant my nafs (soul) piety and purify it, for You are the Best One to purify it (as) You are its Guardian and Master."[1]

[1] Riyad as-Salihin, Book 16 Hadith 15

THE FORERUNNERS

JUZ' 27 | AL-HADĪD

سَابِقُوٓاْ إِلَىٰ مَغْفِرَةٍ مِّن رَّبِّكُمْ وَجَنَّةٍ عَرْضُهَا كَعَرْضِ ٱلسَّمَآءِ وَٱلْأَرْضِ أُعِدَّتْ لِلَّذِينَ ءَامَنُواْ بِٱللَّهِ وَرُسُلِهِۦ ذَٰلِكَ فَضْلُ ٱللَّهِ يُؤْتِيهِ مَن يَشَآءُ وَٱللَّهُ ذُو ٱلْفَضْلِ ٱلْعَظِيمِ ۝

(21) Race toward forgiveness from your Lord and a Garden whose width is like the width of the heavens and earth, prepared for those who believed in Allah and His messengers. That is the bounty of Allah which He gives to whom He wills, and Allah is the possessor of great bounty.

At the beginning of this *Juz'*, we are encouraged to run towards Allāh:

فَفِرُّوٓاْ إِلَى ٱللَّهِ إِنِّى لَكُم مِّنْهُ نَذِيرٌ مُّبِينٌ

So flee to Allāh. Indeed, I am to you from Him a clear warner.
[al-Dhariyāt:50]

Then in Sūrah al-Wāqi'ah, the *sābiqūn* (forerunners) are praised:

وَٱلسَّـٰبِقُونَ ٱلسَّـٰبِقُونَ ۝ أُوْلَـٰٓئِكَ ٱلْمُقَرَّبُونَ

And the forerunners, the forerunners - Those are the ones brought near [to Allāh] [al-Wāqi'ah:10-11]

And then towards the end of the *Juz'*, we are commanded to be of the forerunners:

سَابِقُوٓاْ إِلَىٰ مَغْفِرَةٍ مِّن رَّبِّكُمْ وَجَنَّةٍ عَرْضُهَا كَعَرْضِ ٱلسَّمَآءِ وَٱلْأَرْضِ

Race toward forgiveness from your Lord and a Garden whose width is like the width of the heavens and earth...
[al-Ḥadīd: 21]

We should hasten to those actions that will become a means of our forgiveness and entrance into Paradise. One such action among many others is treading the path of knowledge!

The Prophet ﷺ said,

وَمَنْ سَلَكَ طَرِيقًا يَلْتَمِسُ فِيهِ عِلْمًا سَهَّلَ اللَّهُ لَهُ بِهِ طَرِيقًا إِلَى الْجَنَّةِ

"And whoever follows a path to seek knowledge therein, Allāh will make easy for him a path to Paradise."[1]

May Allāh grant us beneficial knowledge.

---

1   Saḥīḥ Muslim

A SINCERE REPENTANCE
JUZ' 28 | AL-TAHRĪM

يَـٰٓأَيُّهَا ٱلَّذِينَ ءَامَنُوا۟ تُوبُوٓا۟ إِلَى ٱللَّهِ تَوْبَةً نَّصُوحًا عَسَىٰ رَبُّكُمْ أَن يُكَفِّرَ عَنكُمْ سَيِّـَٔاتِكُمْ وَيُدْخِلَكُمْ جَنَّـٰتٍ تَجْرِى مِن تَحْتِهَا ٱلْأَنْهَـٰرُ يَوْمَ لَا يُخْزِى ٱللَّهُ ٱلنَّبِىَّ وَٱلَّذِينَ ءَامَنُوا۟ مَعَهُۥ ۖ نُورُهُمْ يَسْعَىٰ بَيْنَ أَيْدِيهِمْ وَبِأَيْمَـٰنِهِمْ يَقُولُونَ رَبَّنَآ أَتْمِمْ لَنَا نُورَنَا وَٱغْفِرْ لَنَآ ۖ إِنَّكَ عَلَىٰ كُلِّ شَىْءٍ قَدِيرٌ ۝

(8) O you who have believed, repent to Allāh with sincere repentance. Perhaps your Lord will remove from you your misdeeds and admit you into gardens beneath which rivers flow [on] the Day when Allāh will not disgrace the Prophet and those who believed with him. Their light will proceed before them and on their right; they will say, "Our Lord, perfect for us our light and forgive us. Indeed, You are over all things competent."

We are invited to repent to Allāh with a sincere repentance.

A sincere repentance is a means of removal of sins, admittance into Paradise, and light on the Day of Judgment. This light will lead the believers to Paradise.

On the Day of Judgment, just before the *Sirāt* (bridge), people will fall in darkness. Then, each person will be given light according to his deeds. The brightness of the light will be directly proportionate to the level of deeds.

The Prophet ﷺ said, "[On the Day of Judgment] Allāh will give light to each one according to his actions: some of them will be given light like a mountain, proceeding before them; some of them will be given less light than that. Some will be given their light like a date plant, which they will be holding in their hands, and some will be given less than that. The last one to be given light will be given on his big toe, which will shine on and off. When it will shine, he will move forward, and when it will be extinguished he will stand still..."[1]

The Prophet ﷺ said, "Every person, whether hypocrite or believer, will then be given a light that he will use to see his way (on the *Sirāt*). There will be hooks and thorns on the Bridge of Hell that will snatch whomever Allāh wills. The light of the hypocrites will then be extinguished and the believers shall be saved."[2]

When the believers witness the light of the hypocrites being extinguished, they will be concerned for their own light. This is when they will invoke Allāh,

رَبَّنَآ أَتْمِمْ لَنَا نُورَنَا وَٱغْفِرْ لَنَآ ۖ إِنَّكَ عَلَىٰ كُلِّ شَيْءٍ قَدِيرٌ

"Our Lord, perfect for us our light and forgive us. Indeed, You are over all things competent." [al-Taḥrīm: 8]

Let's memorise this *du'ā* and wholeheartedly ask Allāh so that our light is perfected on that Day.

---

1   Saḥīḥ al-Targhīb wal-Tarhīb
2   Saḥīḥ Muslim

NIGHT WORSHIP

JUZ' 29 | AL-MUZZAMMIL

يَـٰٓأَيُّهَا ٱلْمُزَّمِّلُ ۝ قُمِ ٱلَّيْلَ إِلَّا قَلِيلاً ۝ نِّصْفَهُۥ أَوِ ٱنقُصْ مِنْهُ قَلِيلاً ۝ أَوْ زِدْ عَلَيْهِ وَرَتِّلِ ٱلْقُرْءَانَ تَرْتِيلاً ۝ إِنَّا سَنُلْقِى عَلَيْكَ قَوْلاً ثَقِيلاً ۝ إِنَّ نَاشِئَةَ ٱلَّيْلِ هِىَ أَشَدُّ وَطْئًا وَأَقْوَمُ قِيلاً ۝

(1) O you who wraps himself [in clothing], (2) Arise [to pray] the night, except for a little - (3) Half of it - or subtract from it a little (4) Or add to it, and recite the Qur'ān with measured recitation. (5) Indeed, We will cast upon you a heavy word. (6) Indeed, the hours of the night are more effective for concurrence [of heart and tongue] and more suitable for words.

Allāh has singled out the night for extra worship compared to the day. The fact that the revelation of the Qur'ān began at night makes one realise the virtue of night worship. The night time is more specific to build a strong connection with our Lord and draw closer to Him. The silence and peace of the night also allows you to focus better, providing you with a greater opportunity to reflect and grow in wisdom.

Night worship–the way of the righteous before

The Prophet ﷺ said, "Be keen on night prayer as it is the practice of the righteous before you, it is a means of nearness to your Lord, expiation of sins and a barrier against sinning." [1]

The best voluntary worship

The Prophet ﷺ said, "The best prayer after the prescribed prayers is prayer during the night."[2]

Allāh smiles at the one who prays at night

Ibn Mas'ūd ﷺ said, "Our Lord smiles at two men: (one of them is) a man who leaves his mattress and cover, and slips away from his wife and desire, to go and pray. Allāh says, 'O My angels, look at My slave. He has left his mattress and cover and slipped away from his desire and wife to pray, out

---

1   Jami' al-Tirmidhī
2   Saḥīḥ Muslim

of hope for what is with Me
and out of fear of what is with
Me.'"[3]

Acceptance of supplications

The Prophet ﷺ said, "Our
Lord, the Blessed and exalted,
descends to the lowest heaven
every night when a third of the
night remains. He says, 'Who
is calling on Me so that I may
answer him? Who is asking
Me for something so that I may
give to him? Who is asking Me
for forgiveness so that I may
forgive him?'"[4]

Reward for intention!

The Prophet ﷺ said, "Whoever
comes to his bed with the
intention that he will get up to
pray during the night, but is
overcome by sleep and wakes
up when it is morning (*fajr*
time), then what he intended
will be recorded for him and
his sleep is a charity given to
him by his Lord."[5]

So let us make the intention,
InshaAllāh!

O Allāh, help us to remember
You, be grateful to You, and
worship You in the most
excellent manner.

---

3   Saḥīh al-Targhīb
4   Saḥīh Muslim, Book 6 Hadith 201
5   Sunan an-Nasa'i, Book 20 Hadith 190

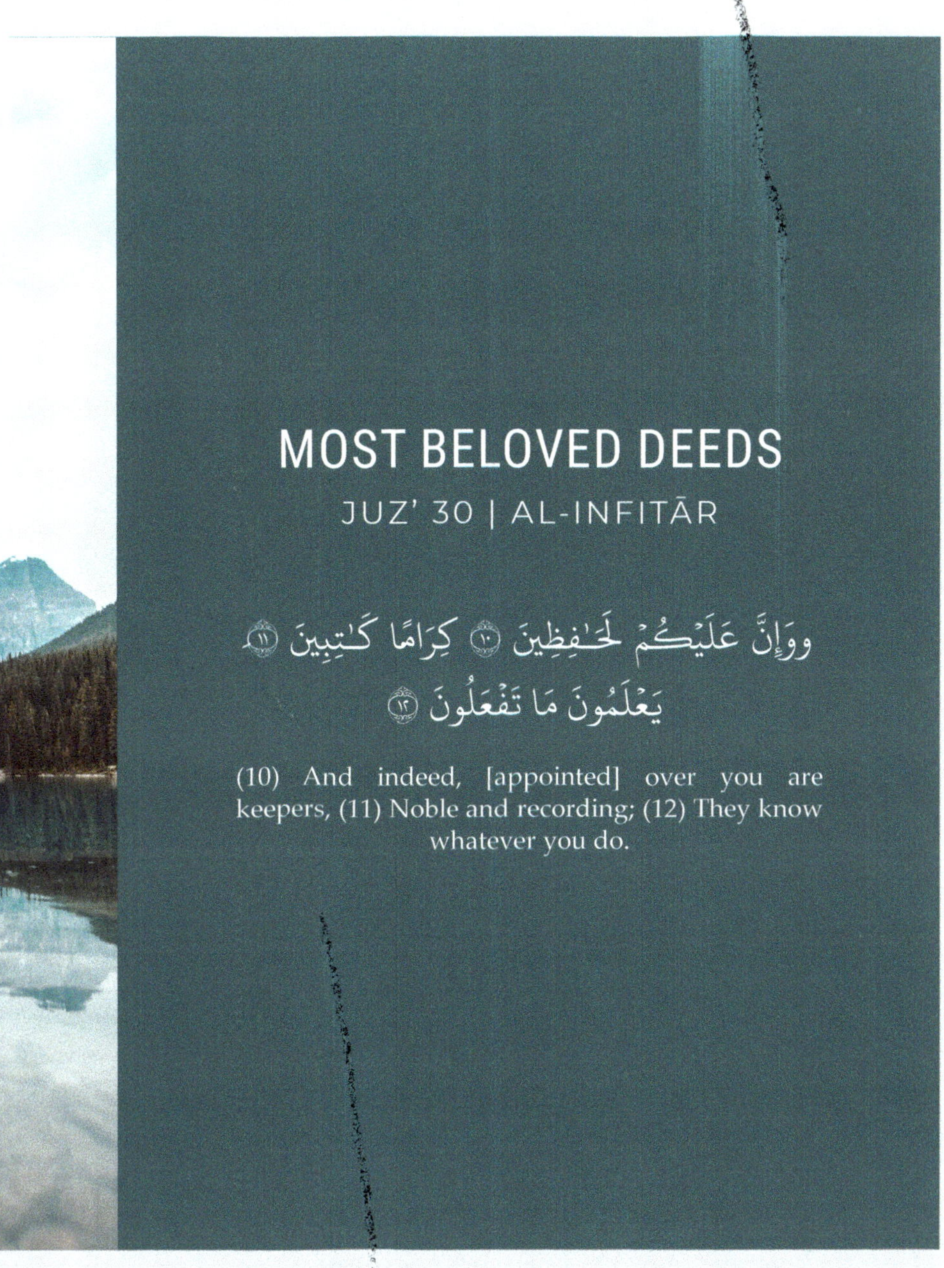

MOST BELOVED DEEDS
JUZ' 30 | AL-INFITĀR

وَإِنَّ عَلَيْكُمْ لَحَفِظِينَ ۝ كِرَامًا كَتِبِينَ ۝ يَعْلَمُونَ مَا تَفْعَلُونَ ۝

(10) And indeed, [appointed] over you are keepers, (11) Noble and recording; (12) They know whatever you do.

The Angels write our words and actions exactly as they are.

The Prophet ﷺ said, "A man said, 'الحمد لله كثيرا *Abundant praise is for Allāh!'* Writing these words became heavy on the angel, so he returned to his Lord concerning this. Allāh said, 'Write it down as My servant said it: 'كثيرا'.'" [1]

The Prophet ﷺ said, "Allāh, the Exalted, said, 'When I test a servant among My believing servants, and he praises Me and is patient over what I test him with, then he will rise from his bed sinless like the day his mother gave him birth.' And the Lord says to the guardian-angels, 'Indeed, I have restricted this servant of mine and tested him, so record for him what you used to record for him of reward before this (test).'" [2]

So when a person consistently does good, but sometimes is unable to do it due to a reason out of his control, he is still rewarded for the good that he used to do. This is why the best deeds are those that are done regularly even if they are little.

The Prophet ﷺ said, "The most beloved deeds to Allāh are those which are done continuously, even if they are little." [3]

---

1   al-Mu'jam al-Awsaṭ
2   as-Silsilah as-Saḥīḥah
3   Saḥīḥ al-Bukhari, Book 81 Hadith 53